Footprints in Shifting Sand
escaping to Seychelles

by
Ron & Gill Gerlach

Phelsuma Press
2015

Phelsuma Press, Cambridge, U.K.

© Ron & Gill Gerlach, 2015

http://wildlife-art.com

ISBN: 978-0-9932203-0-2

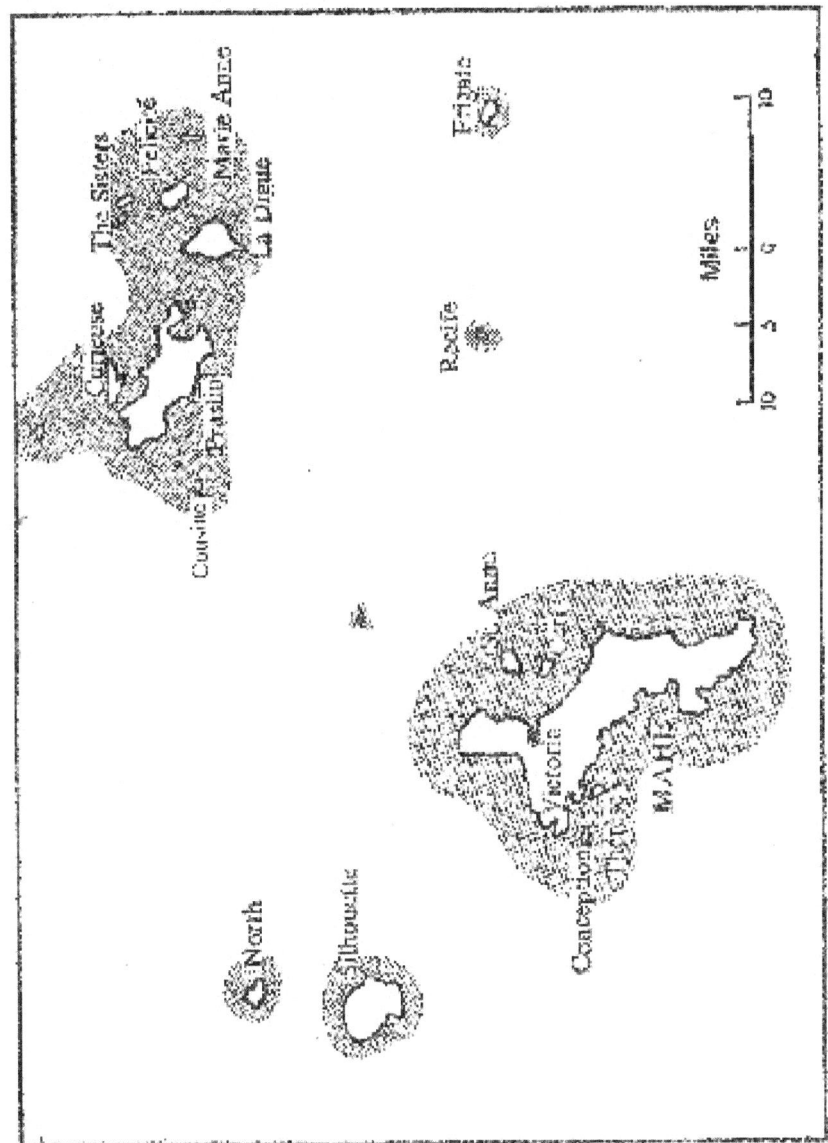

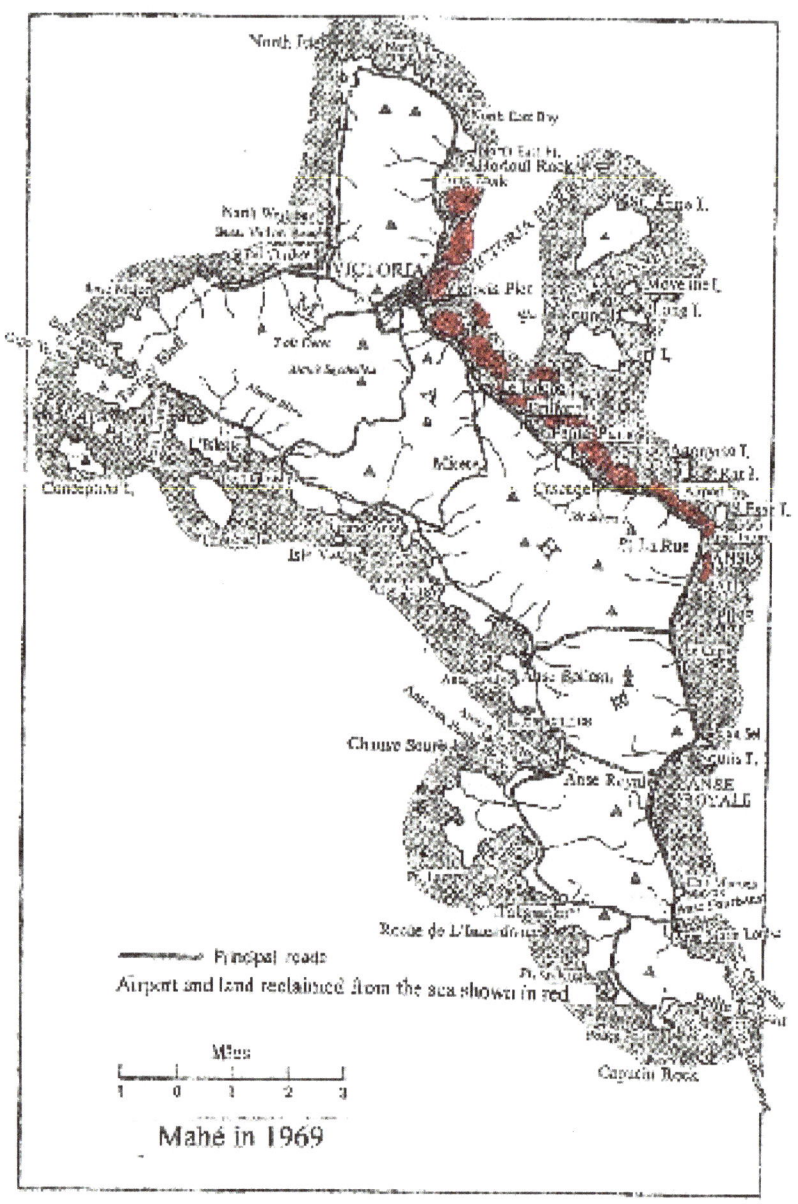

Mahé in 1969

Chapter 1

The Islands
　　The late afternoon light would soon fade to tropical darkness. The islands which for hours had been mere silhouettes began to take on another dimension. These islands, mountain peaks of a sunken land in the vastness of the Indian Ocean, rose from the pale coral sand beaches, through deep green tropical forests to towering granite cliffs. The scent of cinnamon and sun-baked red earth drifted out on the warm evening breeze to the approaching British India steamer *Kampala*.
　　In December 1969 the islands seemed almost uninhabited with only small clusters of low-lying buildings on the very edge of the shore. This dreamy, tranquil haven, a thousand miles from the nearest land, was to be, we dreamt, a brief resting place for our restless spirits – or so we thought at the time.

The Voyage
　　The sea had quite suddenly fallen calm as the ship made its way into the anchorage at Port Victoria, a relief after four days of heaving, twisting and rolling across the turbulent monsoon-driven sea. Our last port of call on the East African coast had been Mombasa. We had spent two days there behaving like tourists, while the ship's cargo was discharged and new cargo and steerage class passengers bound for Karachi and Bombay were taken on.
　　Our touristy outing had taken us up the coast as far as the rustic beach bar called 'White Sands' but our real interest lay in the island town itself. Mombasa, like Zanzibar further down the coast, conjured up images of a romantic past when explorers like Livingstone and Stanley had set out on their ventures into the African interior from these historic Swahili towns. In the sixties, much of Mombasa had been modernised but fragments of the old town were still clustered around Fort Jesus – a reminder of Vasco da Gama's voyage of discovery. The jumble of Arab trading dhows crowded into the old dhow harbour were a living relic of times gone by. These beautiful wooden vessels were a floating market for oriental carpets and perfumes patiently waiting the few months before the steady winds from the south-

east - the trade winds - would carry them back to the Arabian peninsula, loaded with cargoes of spices, timber and, in all likelihood, elephant tusks.

Two days earlier the ship had called at Lourenço Marques, the Maputo of today. 'L.M.' as it was known to the adventurous visitors from neighbouring South Africa, was at that time an exciting destination with wonderful food and wine, no racial segregation, a foreign language - Portuguese - and a range of hotels from the pretty basic to the luxurious and expensive. While the centre of the town was a mixture of modern and traditional Portuguese colonial buildings dominated by an elegant modern cathedral and an interesting botanical garden, the posh end of town was centred around the Polana hotel. Here, the ultra-modern houses were perched on the headland that overlooked the vast expanse of Delagoa Bay and the distant romantic palm-covered island of Inhaca on the very edge of the Indian Ocean.

We had embarked on this voyage to Seychelles in Durban, the largest and most prosperous city on the east coast of Africa. At the time the *S.S. Kampala* and *S.S. Karanja* were the only vessels that made regular trips from Durban to Bombay, calling in at all the ports along the coast and then on to Karachi and finally Bombay. The Seychelles lay conveniently half way between Mombasa and Bombay. In fact this was, in 1969, the only way to travel to these remote tropical islands – the natural choice of these two drifters.

South Africa in the Sixties

We knew Durban fairly well. It had been a holiday destination over the years, an escape from the cold winters on the Highveld around Jo'burg to the sub-tropical climate on the Indian Ocean coast. Strange to think that this thriving city with its busy harbour and bustling tourist trade, its numerous hotels and beachside apartments had blossomed in the heart of the Zulu kingdom but was entirely owned by and existed for white people.

In apartheid South Africa it was not a situation peculiar to Durban; the entire country was subject to the racist regime of 'apart-hate'. This was a political system supported by the great majority of the white inhabitants in a so-called democratic election which excluded all the African, Indian and other non-white inhabitants of the country. It ensured that white people had the freedom to live wherever they chose and to travel to any destination in the country, with the exception of those parts of the cities termed 'locations' for black people, which later became black townships and then black urban areas.

Being African, or Bantu as the authorities liked to say, meant being corralled into controlled areas away from the cities and towns. These aliens in their own country were allowed to be servants and workers in the white-owned towns and suburbs provided they had the necessary permits.

The iniquity of this presumption of white people's birthright only really became obvious when travel and work abroad brought one into contact with the real world - so different from this poisonous political racist dogma.

We met on a bright sunny morning.

It was shortly after I had returned from one of my travels abroad that I first met Gill. I had started work at a small engineering company on the first floor of a building in Loveday Street in Jo'burg. One morning, full of the joys of spring, I breezed into the secretaries' office and was surprised to find a bright-eyed, very attractive young lady, sitting behind one of the desks. Not only was it apparent when she spoke that she was English, she also looked and was dressed like a model straight out of nineteen-sixties Carnaby Street.

I was never good at seeing the whole picture. When it came to the girls in my life, I was easily distracted by beautiful eyes and broad smiles. It never occurred to me to look at hands, fingers and rings. And so, when the invitation to a meal out at Chez André was accepted, it included not only Gill, but also her husband. Despite or because of this shaky start our friendship grew over the next few months.

There were other girls to help make up a foursome and journeys to make on weekends so that we did not die of boredom on those Dutch Reformed church-inspired deadly Sundays in Jo'burg. There was no entertainment – even the cinemas were closed. There was one bookshop in Hillbrow that was open on Sundays and several coffee bars and steakhouses where we could eat and have quiet conversations away from the noise of the badly-behaved children and their screaming parents who inhabited the more popular weekend venues with names like 'Margo's Rainbow Resort'.

There was a way out of these tedious weekends and boring jobs. High adventure and promises of loads of cash were being offered to young men willing to sign up as mercenaries to fight in the civil war in what was then the Belgian Congo. The lure of big money, tied to the risk to life and limb, did not appeal to me, but proved to be an offer that Gill's husband could not resist. When he left, Gill found herself abandoned to her own devices and returned to the life of a single woman. We spent more and more time together and on weekends often went on trips to interesting places out in the African veld. On occasions we spent time at the sailing club on the Vaal river where my sailing dinghy was kept in a primitive rented boat house – more of a shed than a house.

Weekdays saw us both heavily involved in our respective working lives. Gill had an interesting and fulfilling position as a private secretary in a public relations firm. I was trying to juggle a start-up art work business with a school friend at the same time as my rapidly rising position in a large engineering firm. This latter career provided an up-market free car and fuel plus a travel and entertainment expense account which provided a very useful resource for wining and dining out with Gill on many occasions.

Misadventure in Moçambique

We had planned to spend a few days together on Inhaca island where a small reputedly romantic hotel lay hidden in the sub-tropical vegetation. I had managed to get away from work a few days earlier than Gill and had settled in at the hotel. On the first morning after my arrival, a snorkelling party was organised by the hotel and guests set off in a small converted fishing boat to swim and snorkel in the channel where the bay met the open sea. Half a dozen guests, equipped with snorkel and flippers slipped into the warm crystal clear Indian Ocean while the boat took the other guests to the picnic spot on the beach.

Setting out with the snorkelling group, I dived down to have a closer look at a rock cod hiding in a narrow cleft in the rocks. When I surfaced for air, I was startled to find the current had swept me out into the open sea, beyond the breakers and tumbling surf. A sudden flash of memory overcame the growing panic; on a fishing trip with Uncle Ted on the Wild Coast of the Transkei, Ted had explained that where rivers flow into the sea, there is always an eddy on each side which flow back to the shore. Striking out in the direction of the prayed-for eddy, I began to swim parallel to the island's shoreline. The dive boat came out into the open sea searching for their now missing guest but in the heavy sea did not see the frantic 'not waving but drowning' figure struggling away from the current. As I made slow but steady progress towards the island, other worries spurred me on – would all this frantic splashing about on the surface act as a magnet for sharks? After all, these were reputed to be shark-infested waters.

Fortunately the promised sharks failed to materialise, and after what seemed like an eternity, the waves dumped me onto a steep narrow beach, rough with coral and shell fragments but safe and secure after the frightening experience. I lay there dazed and exhausted for some time, the sea still tugging at my feet. I became aware of two African men standing over me, staring at me in silence. They helped me scramble up to the beach-crest and sat with me while I recovered. Eventually one of the men took me by the arm and guided me through the bush to a wide clearing facing the channel between the island and mainland. There I saw the boat tied to a tree in a small sheltered cove and the hotel guests spread out on the towels, sunbathing and enjoying a picnic. They seemed unperturbed by what had happened but were relieved to see the bedraggled drowning victim alive and walking.

A raging earache put an end to any hope of a quiet recovery during the night. Mother's remedy of putting a teaspoonful of warm olive oil in the offending ear only made things worse. It transpired that a badly torn eardrum had allowed both olive oil and coral fragments to enter the inner ear. This was all dealt with in hospital after an emergency flight from Lourenço Marques to Jo'burg.

Changing priorities

In the long quiet nights in hospital, an underlying sense of unease took root. Was this long drawn out life of materialism stretching from one's twenties to old age really what life was all about? There was a mindless weariness about this way of life. The people we most admired, the writers, artists and craftsmen, were those who lived their lives outside this universal lust for money and possessions.

With these thoughts shared with Gill and the imminent return of her disillusioned warrior from the Belgian Congo, more Agamemnon than Ulysses, we had to put our friendship on hold.

Discharged from hospital, I began to divest myself of my material possessions. I sold the sports car and sailing boat and, much to the chagrin of my parents, gave all else away. I managed to withdraw from the fledgling artwork business without too much acrimony. Then, back at the paying job, I went to see Arnold the project manager, a romantic dreamer who had often said that he was fed-up with his boring life and dreamed of the freedom of living on board the yacht he kept moored on the Moçambique coast. I parked myself on a corner of his cluttered desk and said, "If you are really serious about sailing around the world, I'm your man!"

Gill, meanwhile, was planning to leave South Africa and hoping for a job somewhere interesting in Europe. Returning on the Union Castle Line 'Windsor Castle' from Durban to Southampton she spent some time with family and friends in England before leaving again for three years in Switzerland, first at La Tour de Peilz on Lake Geneva and later in Geneva with one of the many international organisations in that cosmopolitan town. An advertisement for an English-speaking secretary to work on a large estancia – a cattle ranch – in the south of Brazil in Santa Catarina province proved too interesting to ignore and she sailed from Genoa to Rio on the first stage of the trip which involved a flight from Rio to Curitiba where she was met by the rancher and his family – there for an important cattle show – before a long drive to the ranch.

Work involved general secretarial duties and taking down the dictation of a variety of short stories which the boss invented from day to day – these were sent off to various American magazines and were generally accepted for publication. It was an extremely beautiful part of the world – rolling acres of pampas and a horse 'Rosita' to ride whenever she felt like it. But it was a remote and isolated existence and one which did not appeal for the long term.

Sailing into the unknown

An Afrikaner friend of Arnold's who had some leave due offered us the exotic transport to Inhambane in Mozambique where the *Uzulane* was moored. We settled in for the long drive in his huge Ford Galaxy with its fashionable fishtails the size of two killer whale dorsal fins and its questionable luxurious plastic leopard-skin print seat covers.

Inhambane lay about half way between L.M. and Beira. The small village served as a ferry point for crossing the estuary some kilometres inland. A quiet haven of peace with silent sailing dhows ferrying passengers across the water, dependent only on the daylight and the ebb and flow of the tides.

We spent two months 'messing about in boats'. We parked the *Uzulane* up against the jetty at spring low tide and scraped the years of old seaweed growth from her metal hull. We checked the sails, replaced the rigging and fuelled up the engine. On a rising tide, we slipped our mooring and, using the engine, made our way down the length of the estuary. At high tide we were faced with crossing the roaring surf into the open sea. Thirty minutes later, the boat tossed by turbulent waves, Arnold panicked, went to pieces, and demanded that we turn back to the safety of Inhambane. That proved to be the only time we ventured out into the open sea. After that, we primarily propped up the local bars and hung about doing nothing – as meaningless an existence as the materialism we thought we had escaped.

I had secreted a small box of water colour paints in my bag and at times, escaping from the booze, indulged myself by making rough finger-painted sketches – there were no brushes in the box. There were times too when I retreated into the pages of Radnakrishnan's book on 'The Hindu Way of Life'.

Towards the end of the second month Arnold's wife and daughter turned up to plead with him to come to his senses but he would not budge. He didn't tell them about our abortive maiden voyage and his panic attack. It was obvious that he wasn't going anywhere. The atmosphere soured to the point where my only prospect of going anywhere was to share the driving with Arnold's wife on the long journey down the coast to L.M., through Swaziland and the Natal coast to Durban.

An alternative route to freedom

On the very first morning in Durban, a large poster featuring a sunny beach and dreamy over-hanging palms drew my attention. It was an advertisement for British India Lines, extolling the delights of spending time in the Seychelles on the passage from Durban to Bombay. Seychelles, the islands of love and romance, islands lost in the vastness of the Indian Ocean.

British India Lines operated the two vessels between Africa and India: the *Karanja* and the *Kampala*; the Eastern Shipping Co. operated the *State of Bombay*, known in Seychelles as 'The State of Decay'. Two birds with one stone then: a stay in paradise and a chance to encounter first-hand the wonders of the Hindu way of life.

A first encounter with paradise

This was to be the first of several passages up the East African coast on the *S.S. Kampala* as she made her way from port to port as far as Mombasa and then headed out on the thousand mile leg to Seychelles. She carried first and cabin class passengers and a teeming hold of steerage class Indian travellers but her main activity was moving cargo from port to port.

There was an old world colonial charm about the passenger accommodation and staterooms. The passengers were a bit like that too – elderly ex-colonial employees, colonial staff full of their own self-importance and an few stragglers including two elderly South African men intent on finding themselves some free love on the islands. Among the first class passengers was a well-off South African couple with a gorgeous daughter. And then there was Andrew, or, as he preferred to be called, Andy. He hadn't spent much time in South Africa, having been brought up in Kenya. A free spirit with seemingly no direction in his life, his large frame and over-exuberant nature were the perfect disguise for his insecurity.

Seychelles was as perfect as any dream could be. Palm-fringed beaches lapped by crystal clear warm seas; mountains rising steeply from the sea, covered in dense tropical forest. The capital of the islands, Victoria, on the largest island, Mahé was a mere crossroads dominated by a few colonial style buildings and by a clock tower; about twenty feet tall and suffering from many years of peeling Public Works Department silver paint, this was capped with an oversized and unsteady weather-vane and a number of lamps on unevenly bent brackets. The people were a mixture of African, Indian, Chinese and European with an upper crust of what were known as 'Grands Blancs' or descendants of the original French colonial settlers, and all under the benign

gaze of the British colonial staff. I whiled away two months on the islands, dreaming, trying to write and generally being drawn into this slow, lazy way of life. The first month at the Hotel des Seychelles, the most expensive hotel on the island's best beach, Beau Vallon, cost less than £2 per day, full board. When the South African couple and their beautiful daughter left, I moved for my second month to a small chalet overlooking Northolme hotel at a slightly cheaper rate.

Andy, it turned out, had family living in Seychelles and during that second month introduced me to his mother, Gisèle and her partner, Knud. There were several long boozy evenings spent listening to their adventurous lives in Africa and exploits in Kenya's 'Happy Valley' (the expatriate community of colonial staff, aristocratic dropouts and big game hunters, dedicated to fast living, wife-swapping, and money troubles, all under the influence of limitless alcohol) and being entertained by Andy with his permanent grin and easy laugh.

Hotel des Seychelles
BEAU VALLON
Cables: " Idyllic " Seychelles   Post Office Box 146, Victoria, Mahé, Seychelles

ONLY at the HOTEL DES SEYCHELLES are ALL the following amenities GENUINELY AVAILABLE:
* PRIVATE BUNGALOWS FACING THE SEA
* SMALL CARS FOR HIRE AT REASONABLE RENTALS
* BEACHSIDE COCKTAIL BAR (the Goggle and Flipper !)
* CHARMING LOUNGES AND RESIDENTS' BAR IN THE HOTEL
* WELL-STOCKED PRIVATE LIBRARY
* LARGE SELECTION OF HI-FI MUSIC
* TENNIS COURT   (but only when you want it !)
* THE BEST AVAILABLE CUISINE
and for the sea:
LUXURY FISHING CRUISER
FULL DEEP-SEA FISHING EQUIPMENT
COURTEOUS AND EXPERIENCED COXSWAIN AND BOAT CREW
ALL NECESSARY GOGGLING EQUIPMENT
SIX SMALL BOATS
SURF BOARDS, WATER SKIS AND LI-LOS
SPEEDBOAT FOR AQUAPLANING AND WATER SKIING
NEW 12-SEATER MINIBUS FOR TOURS AND PARTIES

Without wishing to appear lyrical, which we should not do, since Seychelles is a simple place, IT IS a grand place. We hope you will enjoy living here as much as we enjoy helping you to have what we hope will turn out to be a HOLIDAY YOU WILL REMEMBER.

La Digue

During my second month there was an excursion to another of the Seychelles islands. Knud had some interest in a schooner being built on La Digue and asked me to make exact measurements of its hull. The journey to La Digue started at the seaward end of the Long Pier where all the island schooners were berthed. Looking somewhat out of place among these sailing boats was the ferry to Praslin, the second largest island. This ferry, the *Lady Esmé*, was an unprepossessing motor launch rumoured to have a design fault in that she had an almost flat bottom, not best suited to rough seas. The two hour journey had to be timed so that the arrival on Praslin allowed enough time to get to the twice weekly 'Doctor's boat' to La Digue.

This island, so quiet, so peaceful, so calm, seemed as though it could only exist in the imagination. The onset of the south-east trade-wind sighing through the casuarina trees, ruffling the coconut palm fronds, sent lazy waves hushing up coral white-sand beaches from a crystal clear sun-dappled sea.

The only accommodation available to visitors to the island was in the government guesthouse – two small rooms separated by a covered verandah, with a cold shower and toilet marooned in the garden. Fortunately Madame Moustache, whose husband was the boat builder, offered to provide meals for a small charge. Although there were several hundred islanders, it seemed as though the island was uninhabited. In three days, a couple of bicycles and a solitary ox-cart passed the boatyard; it was rumoured that the only two motor vehicles on the island, a mini which had been converted into a pick-up, and a dumper, had collided head-on and were out of action.

All too soon it all came to an end and it was time to board the Karanja again and set off for Karachi and then finally – Bombay.

India

And then there was India.

Ah! India.

Bombay, the monumental Gateway to India and the splendid Taj hotel. It was all so different, it even smelled exotic. The very first person who tugged at my sleeve as I stepped out of the door of a small modest hotel was a ragged, bearded little man – an Anglo Indian, he said - called Sam. He acted as a self-appointed guide and counsellor for the next few days. Sam provided some protection from the beggars and traders who thronged the overcrowded noisy streets of Bombay where the scent of spices wafting on the air was more often overpowered by the smell of human waste.

Sam insisted that the train journey to New Delhi should not be compromised by travelling first class. "Take luxury class, it only costs a few rupees more – other class no good for gentlemen." After the pressing, plucking crowds, the train journey was in fact a luxury, a brief few hours of being treated like royalty.

The countryside was parched and dusty in this pre-monsoon season. The few inhabitants, dust-covered in dusty bedraggled clothes trudged alongside rickety animal-drawn carts.

I stayed in a more upmarket hotel in Delhi with kind and considerate staff. They helped organise a private taxi tour down to Agra to visit the Taj Mahal, the tranquil, beautiful masterpiece of one man's love for his wife, and the only time I felt at peace in this crowded country.

With the return to Delhi and its crowded streets teeming with people, traffic and scrawny half-starved cows, came a sense of utter hopelessness and depression. What was it that had brought me to this pushing, shoving, sleeve-plucking poverty-stricken country? Was this really a way to the understanding of human dignity – the way to a life that did not wallow in materialism? Even the lure of a visit to the Buddhi tree where the Buddha attained enlightenment could not overcome this need to escape. There followed a long train journey to Calcutta; hours and hours lying on a bunk in a compartment with five other recumbent passengers behind a barred window.

The Black Hole of Calcutta was a phrase we had grown up with, describing anywhere dark and gloomy. And Calcutta really was the black hole into which all hope disappeared. One brief excursion into the city with its millions of inhabitants including countless thousands crowed into squatter cities made of cardboard boxes, ended in a return to the hotel and not venturing out again until the taxi-ride to the airport and a flight to Bangkok.

Thailand proved to be the perfect antidote. Yes, it was busy and crowded in places, but the quiet gentle dignity and warm welcoming smiles could melt even the hardest heart. There followed a few brief days in Hong Kong and then a long sea voyage on the P & O *Oriana* around Australia, across the Indian Ocean and back to South Africa. A few weeks later, in answer to an offer of work in Seychelles, I boarded the Karanja on its journey to the islands – a thousand miles from anywhere.

Island life

In long letters to Gill, I described how a strange vessel looking like a cross between a cargo lighter and an amateur- built greenhouse had come alongside the *Kampala* as soon as she dropped anchor. This plying boat, as it was known, brought on board the immigration, police, dignitaries if needed and hotel representatives. It then ferried the officials and passengers to the 'long pier' – a road that had been built on the reef flat, stretching from almost the centre of Victoria out to the edge of the reef where small boats could tie up.

Waiting in one of the grey buildings that housed the port office and warehouses was Andy, ready to deliver bear hugs and backslaps and an invitation to a meeting the next day with Knud in the offices of the Seychelles Development Company to discuss terms of employment. Here, Knud was assisted by a middle-aged Scot called Helen. Terms and conditions were agreed and the offer accepted of free accommodation in a newly refurbished house at Sancta Maria in the south of the island.

There was an invitation to dinner that evening at their home at Sans Soucis, situated high up on the mountainside with breathtaking views of the town and a seascape of scattered islands surrounding the anchorage and then away as far as the islands of La Digue and Praslin. Theirs was a rambling unremarkable house which had previously played host to Archbishop Makarios of Cyprus, exiled to Seychelles in 1956 for his alleged support of the terrorist campaign against British rule in Cyprus. The house, situated in well-tended extensive gardens, contained some pieces of antique furniture which Gisèle and Knud had brought with them – this gave the house an air of grace and a feeling of permanence. On their arrival in Seychelles, this furniture had been transported across the island and deposited on the verandah of the small chalet at the Hotel des Seychelles where its owners were staying prior to renting the house at Sans Soucis. While Knud was at work, Gisèle socialised with the other hotel guests; among them was Noel Coward, who would appear on the verandah in tears of frustration at his sleepless nights, constantly kept awake by the nearby frogs. Stranded between ships, he was hating every moment of his enforced stay on the over-heated remote tropical island.

Knud was a tall, handsome and distinguished-looking Dane who spoke English without a trace of accent. Gisèle was Belgian, brought up in England where her father was a diplomat. She spoke fluent French and perfect English, of the BBC style of the 1940s. Strikingly attractive, a look-alike for Ava Gardner, she was always elegantly dressed and made-up. She was a bubbly, enthusiastic hostess who never showed a ruffled feather. Although they had come to Seychelles from England, like many expats on the islands at the time they were really 'out of Africa' – upper-class misfits moving on from adventurous lives in Kenya, Tanganyika, Rhodesia and Somalia. Andy, with his big heart, wide smile and endless laughter, was the son of Gisèle's earlier marriage to an Englishman and he had survived to tell the tale of his insecure past.

My job was to manage the site office, construction staff and development project and to deal with prospective owners of building sites at Anse á la Mouche on the main island. This was the first property development project in Seychelles, set up by someone in England selling dreams to unsuspecting buyers who were looking for an island in the sun. The main preoccupation at the time was to lay out and build the roads that would service the properties. Knud, who was showing less and less inclination to leave the security of his office as though developing some form of agoraphobia, despite the beauty of his surroundings, was keen to teach me the elements of surveying. It was all about geometry: triangles and arithmetic and wandering around in the bush with two men, a tape measure and a theodolite, which appealed to me but the physical work was no longer of interest to Knud.

For several months the work was interesting and quite fulfilling, surveying and cutting roads among the palms and the at times quite challenging virgin landscape of the hillside at Sailfish Estate. There was an old Land-Rover that served as a workhorse on the still-to-be-made-up roads and to get to meetings on the surfaced roads to Victoria.

The house at Sancta Maria was one of only two houses standing high on the hillside overlooking the wide, shallow bay of Anse á la Mouche. It looked down on the coastal flat where the land to be developed was still part of a coconut plantation. At night the only sounds were the chuckling of the geckos and songs of insects, the darkness interrupted by only one small spot of light at the isolated farm. Andy had moved in, occupying one of the guest rooms. Gisèle had insisted on installing a maid to do the housework and cooking. Life was cheap; a metre-long yellow-fin tuna cost the equivalent of fifty pence and provided healthy meals for a week. There was an old fisherman who came by occasionally with a bucket of oysters he had prised off the reef, which we ate standing at the sink in the kitchen. Andy had somehow managed to get the use of a small boat and outboard engine which was used on perfect calm evenings for trips out to sea to catch fish and to lounge about in, gazing at the setting sun and rising stars – that sudden tropical transition.

One unforgettable evening, Andy and I were persuaded by Gisèle to attend the amateur dramatic society's production by members of the colonial service of 'The Importance of Being Earnest'. Gisèle wanted 'her young men' to show their good breeding and taste. She insisted that formal dress was necessary, resulting in the pair of us arriving at the Seychelles College theatre attired in tropical formal evening dress, known as 'Red Sea Kit'. This originated as an adaptation of formal evening dress for Royal Navy officers in the Red Sea where the heat and humidity made normal evening dress impractical. It later spread to expatriate communities in the Middle East and Far East and consisted of a white shirt, black trousers and bow-tie plus a red cummerbund to temper the informal look. So there we were, thus attired amongst an audience of colonial staff in short-sleeved shirts and slacks.

This life all began to come unstuck with the arrival of the first property owners – or, at least, that is what they thought they were. Their first visit after the long air and sea voyage was to the office where they were shown a beautiful artist's layout of the development and a selection of British designed bungalows that, it was said, would become the tropical island homes they dreamed of.

I collected them from the Hotel des Seychelles after lunch and drove them across the most scenic route to the embryonic development. We drove along winding roads through lush tropical vegetation, climbing up and down sculptured granite cliffs, a different vista around every bend and everywhere, the brilliant clear blues of the sea. All this led to the Estate: no roads as yet, no water, no lighting and more often than not, a piece of land on the edge of the wide coastal marsh with its more than welcoming mosquitos. Seeing their disappointment and bearing the brunt of their anger, it soon became obvious why Knud was so agoraphobic!

He, it turned out, was not too happy about the premature sale of the land but needed the job. I, on the other hand, didn't need to have angry visitors yelling at me every other day, and decided to pack it in.

Down a precipitous half-made road on the north of the island, I found a temporary refuge in the half-built, half-run Carana Beach hotel, sort-of managed by an elderly lady called Mme. Corgat. The so-called hotel consisted of ten bungalows, most of them unfurnished, probably because the owner had run out of money. They stood like soldiers in formation on a terrace overlooking the cove which was embraced by two rocky headlands, one of which, Cap Soleil, was owned by Knud. The only other sometime resident was a pretty young Seychelloise girl who, according to a whispered confidentiality from Mme Corgat, belonged to Mr. Bill Pomeroy, a rich American – an implied warning? One of the small bungalows perched on the slope above a dramatic secluded bay provided the antidote to the angry scenes of the past few months and a chance to get back to writing long letters to Gill at her haven in Switzerland. Some days there were long walks around the north of the island, all the way to Beau Vallon and the Goggle and Flipper bar for a beer or two with Andy.

Among the footloose young expats who thought they were passing through Seychelles but stayed on instead, Andy had found two Swiss lads who gave him the chance once again to smoke a few joints. Vladimir and Jean-Pierre were friends too with some young Americans who rented a strange house built around a tumble of rocks at Danzil where evenings were spent somewhat in the way of the descriptions in a Jack Kerouac novel: boozing, smoking the odd joint and putting the world to rights.

After one such visit, I took a joint back with me to my hideout at Carana beach and spent a lazy afternoon marvelling in that befuddled state at the beauty of the passing clouds. The following day the clouds were still drifting by, but without clouds of smoke in the brain they seemed brighter and offered the possibility of rain and physical refreshment rather than some confused smoke induced daydream.

It was time to move on.

The free-living on the island continued for a short while until Andy got himself into deep water at a posh cocktail evening he attended because Gisèle wanted to show the higher end of society what a serious young man he was. During the evening, wanting to liven things up a little, Andy offered a pot-laden cigarette to the rather stiff and humourless Attorney General of the colonial service. He looked eccentric enough, and with Andy helping him to spread his new-found bonhomie and laughter among the crowd, seemed to be having a whale of a time, but wasn't mightily pleased when the high wore off. It took all of Gisèle's diplomatic efforts to persuade the authorities to let Andy take the next boat to Mombasa and a flight to London. The alternative would have been jail.

Together for a short while

I, meanwhile, had travelled to Switzerland to spend a few weeks with Gill and to tell her of my latest hare-brained scheme to join an American, whom I had met in Seychelles, to finish building a yacht in Thailand and sail it around the world. He had decided that the then trendy approach was to use the world's least buoyant material to construct the hull - concrete! He assured me that there were a number of successful concrete yachts that actually floated, and partly allayed my scepticism by reminding me that steel is also not know for its buoyancy. Gill was in the process of being transferred to Italy to work in the office in Genoa. The happy few weeks came to an end too soon and I could stop trying to out-macho the suave young Italian men who were hovering around Gill.

A spoke in the wheel

American Frank lived in a small town known to the Americans as Korat, in central Thailand. He worked for a company supplying the war effort in neighbouring Vietnam. He lived in a house attached to a small artisanal silk factory which gave me the opportunity to watch the extraction and spinning of the silk, the dyeing process and the eventual weaving into lengths of beautifully coloured silk fabric. Fascination with the silk works helped to overcome the boredom of hanging around waiting for Frank to have enough spare time to visit the 'ship yard' where the hull of the yacht had been cast.

Eventually the journey to Pattaya materialised; a journey through the beautiful Thai countryside, away from the calming shuttle noises of the silk factory and the far-too-frequent roar of the bombers as they took off and returned to the nearby airfield. Pattaya with its street market and beautiful beach was mostly peopled by American forces on rest and recuperation from Vietnam.

There was a disaster waiting at the so-called shipyard which was more like a shambolic construction site. The concrete hull of the yacht had been cast with the keel uppermost and two large wooden wheels had been built around the hull to allow it to be slowly rolled over into an upright position. As the hull was being rolled, a spoke of one of the wheels snapped and punched a huge hole in the concrete – a disaster beyond repair.

With the project now abandoned and all my savings spent, I decided to head off to Australia to find work. In those days, a clean chest X-ray was the only paperwork required to get through immigration and to have the opportunity to settle or work.

I spent six unsatisfactory months working in Sydney and had time at the end of my stay to make a week's excursion to New Zealand where the spectacular scenery and tranquillity of the South island almost persuaded me to become a shepherd and spend my days contemplating something or other in this majestic landscape of beautiful valleys and mountains. There couldn't have been a greater contrast between that mountainous landscape and the bus ride from Sydney to Perth that crossed the totally flat, kangaroo-less waste of the 400 miles across the Nullabore Plain on the way to Perth. Perth with its nearby port of Freemantle was the start of another sea passage across the Indian Ocean to Capetown.

<u>Leaving it all behind</u>

Travellers cheques and savings reduced to rubble, I returned to my parents' home on the southern outskirts of Jo'burg. Mom was happy to have her son at home again but Dad, who had grown accustomed to the peace and quiet since sisters Rhona and Ann had settled down and now had their own families, was not well pleased.

Seeking work with meaning and a more aesthetic vision than the purely utilitarian dreariness of engineering, I took a very junior, low paid design job in a large architectural firm. I was soon to discover that all the bright young people with their dreams and enthusiasm were part of a publicity machine that had less to do with architecture and more to do with marketing the architectural firm.

Out of the blue came a request from Gill to help her out of a compromising situation on the ranch in Brazil. Fortunately there were sufficient savings in the bank to pay for a one way ticket from Rio to Jo'burg. Gill moved into a flat with three friends overlooking Joubert Park in the centre of the city. I continued living at home but over the following months, weekends were spent travelling around the country in sister Ann's little Austin A35.

One long weekend, we went back to Moçambique. It was a chance to enjoy the good Portuguese-inspired food and visit some earlier haunts but avoiding Inhaca island this time around. We did however, spend one night at Xai-Xai, a favourite beach resort for many tourists. We found a fairly rough campsite not far from the smart hotels and set about erecting our rather small tent. As the sun set, dark clouds rose from the surrounding vegetation.

Dark clouds of mosquitoes, nasty zinging little demons - it was a memorable mosquito-ridden night; we ended up collapsing the tent over us to reduce flying space for the little devils and used the small mesh-covered vent of the two-man tent as a breathing hole. We managed to get a little sleep in our very friendly confined space, but were delighted to see a mosquito free sunrise the next morning.

Moçambique was also a place of respite from the oppressive apartheid racial laws in South Africa. In the previous few months we had been more aware of the conflicting choices faced by young liberal-minded whites. One evening, returning from a visit to a friend who had crossed the most dangerous apartheid law by having a child with an Indian lover, we did what was considered to be an absolute taboo. We stopped on a lonely dark stretch of road to offer a lift to a black man whose car had broken down. He turned out to be the editor of the popular African magazine called 'Drum'. It was he who told us about Steve Biko and his belief that the anti-apartheid struggle needed to be driven by the blacks, not the white liberals.

Shortly afterwards, a number of plain-clothes security people visited Gill's flat and questioned her about her movements in previous months. Fortunately this was based on a mis-identification on their part; it transpired that they were looking for someone with the same name, or so they said. Fortunately they hadn't noticed the Che Guevara books on the shelf. It was an unsettling encounter and finally persuaded us to look for greener, less traumatic pastures.

There was a way for us to escape the shackles of employment – we could put our artistic talents to use. Gill had an innate sense of colour and I could draw and paint. We thought carefully about the difficulty that prospective buyers would have transporting paintings on aircraft, or even by sea, and decided that batik paintings on cloth were a better option – a batik could be folded up and creased and only needed to be ironed to remove the creases. If the batiks didn't sell, there was still the option of paintings (however difficult to transport) or maybe even the possibility of setting up a pottery to make use of the claylike red earth of the islands.

I resigned from the architectural practice and spent the last month learning the basics of pottery in a small pottery works while, in the evenings, blocking up the sink in Gill's flat with wax as I tried to master the craft of batik-making.

Gill spent these last few months as a private secretary to the boss of L'Oréal, the French hair-care products company. It was unnerving to discover that their up-market hair preparations were mixed and quality tested in an old bath-tub in a back room of their tiny offices.

That was how we came to be standing on the deck of the *Kampala* as she slowly made her way into the anchorage between St. Anne island and Mahé. The lights of the tiny capital of Seychelles, Victoria, were slowly being switched on in the rapidly falling dusk.

Chapter 2

Return to Paradise

There was a short but slow journey in the 'plying boat' between the ship and the shore. The Chief of Police had come aboard the *Kampala* to check our passports and we had met Raymonde and agreed to stay at her Beach Hotel. In the baggage shed at the end of the long pier we were welcomed by a smiling Gerry Robert – one of my work colleagues on my earlier stay – eager to drive us over the island to the hotel. As the car negotiated the steep winding mountain road, for Gill this first encounter with an inky black tropical night, illuminated only by a pair of out-of-focus headlamps that lit either dry stone walls or sheer unprotected precipices, was a nerve-shattering introduction to life on a desert island.

The Beach Hotel, however, turned out to be a haven of peace and tranquillity. The reception area, bar and restaurant were all housed in what looked like an over-large traditional boathouse; the accommodation a row of small but comfortable self-contained rooms. Raymonde, a striking-looking blonde, brim full of exuberance, fussed over us until we were settled in, fed and sent to bed for the night.

Raymonde's Beau Vallon Beach Hotel

We woke next morning to a cloudless blue sky, palm trees leaning over the small cove, Silhouette island lying on the distant horizon, the sea as calm and tranquil as a lake. After the heaving seas of our three-week journey, Gill was struggling to come to terms with the solid ground which seemed still to be rolling steadily.

We had a busy week ahead of us. Our immediate need

The original Beach Hotel with its long-established reputation for friendly atmosphere, courteous service and good food.

All rooms overlook the sea and have their own showers and toilets, and verandas giving direct access to sandy beaches, safe bathing and a shallow lagoon ideal for small children.

For a carefree holiday come to

RAYMONDE'S
BEAU VALLON BEACH HOTEL
Fully licensed
Proprietors: MRS. RAYMONDE DONKIN

was to cash in the remaining part of our tickets from Seychelles to India (can you imagine trying to do that today?) which netted us the princely sum of fifty pounds. We kept this windfall to pay for somewhere to stay once our paid-for week at the Beach Hotel came to an end. We were fortunate that Raymonde knew of an elderly Englishman who had a small house to let. Harry lived a short distance from the hotel in an old wooden Creole-style house with its wide verandah and spacious airy rooms where the walls did not meet the roof, allowing the air to circulate through the entire house.

A retired colonial servant from Kenya, Harry had settled down in this peaceful paradise far, far away from the troubled Mau-Mau times in Africa. He lived alone except for the permanent live-in maid, and was usually to be found resting in his favourite deckchair. He was a little apologetic about the house he had for rent.

Lyons Corner House, as Harry called it, was pretty basic but was clean and within our limited budget. The house was equipped with some rudimentary furniture, including an iron double bed with a coir (coconut fibre) mattress and, in the kitchen alcove, a two-burner paraffin cooker, cold water and no fridge.

The tiny garden was enclosed by a dense hedge that sheltered the property from the sharp bend in the road and from the neighbours across the way who put their ghetto-blaster on the road edge on the weekends, so that all the neighbourhood could listen to Jim Reeves.

In the days prior to our move to the salubrious Lyons Corner House, I had a chance to introduce Gill to Knud and Gisèle, two people who would become a most important part of our lives on the islands over the next thirty years. Gisèle took us under her wing like a

mother hen. We were the same age as her own two children and our presence and unstable lives made us her substitute family – to fuss over and worry about.

Knud was trying to adapt to the rapidly diminishing interest in the property development business. It was a time when the British government enforced a limit of fifty pounds per annum that holiday-makers could take abroad and the fallout was the cutting-back on what was seen as the extravagant lifestyle of the Anse la Mouche development's director and his wife. They no longer lived at the splendid Sans Soucis house. He was still based in his office in the Mahé Trading building while he and secretary Helen wound up their part of the property development business prior to its being recapitalised and put under new management.

At one of the many cocktail parties that they had given at Sans Soucis before being down-graded, Knud and Gisèle had met another aspiring property developer who was building houses and a hotel in the north of the island of Mahé at Glacis. He had mentioned to Knud that there were no private sector engineers and that the Public Works Department were unwilling to take on private work. This engineering vacuum was a happy coincidence for us, as we soon realised that it would take time to get any craftwork underway and we stood little chance of living the rest of our lives on our fifty pounds.

With the prospect of a steady income on offer, we settled down to our new life at Lyons Corner House. We grew accustomed to the neighbours' weekend musical extravaganzas and the often torrential monsoon rain thundering down on the tin roof. It was, however, mostly quiet and peaceful.

There was a painfully thin old man, clad in khaki shirt and baggy shorts, who appeared on the roadside every other day with a large basket of freshly baked bread rolls. Other supplies could be found in a small 'duka' nearby and fresh fish was available on the beach when the sound of a fisherman blowing into a conch shell announced the arrival of the catch. Fresh milk, however, was reserved for the wives and children of the colonial staff although it occasionally turned up at the duka in Amstel beer bottles with stoppers cut from coconut husk. For the most part, people used evaporated milk.

More complicated supplies came from Victoria and were generally combined with a trip to the bank, post office and the public library. This involved catching a bus to the capital or being lucky enough to be at the bus stop when Major Reid or Mrs. Wakeford were en route to town and would pick us up and give us a lift. The buses, which were covered lorries, known locally as 'camions', were privately owned and ran a more or less regular service.

Each morning the owner fitted hard wooden benches into the back of the camion and set off to work in Victoria. He stopped at designated stops to collect passengers. When the passengers were deposited in the town, the driver set off to do his morning's work. On his way home for lunch, passengers returned home. In order to get him to stop along the return route, it was necessary to yell "Débark" as loudly as possible. After the driver had had his lunch break, he repeated the service in the afternoon. It worked most of the time and no-one minded the baskets of vegetables, 'packets' of mackerel carried on a loop made of coconut frond, or the live poultry tied together by their legs.

Once a week there was the excitement of a visit to the nearby Hotel des Seychelles where the lounge was rearranged to accommodate the travelling cinema on its tour around the districts. It was sheer luxury to sit in comfy seats, beer in hand as a film was projected onto a wind-blown sheet.

On Christmas Eve we decided to blow some of our remaining funds on Northolme Hotel's Christmas dinner. This involved booking some days in advance and, in our case, walking to the hotel in the inky blackness. We arrived in good time, very hungry and somewhat tired after the uphill walk, only to discover that the Governor of Seychelles was to appear for dinner.

Unfortunately as it was to be a formal dinner, laid out on one long table, it was inevitable that we should have to await the arrival of this guest of 'honour' who was, after all, in Seychelles to represent the Queen. We were quite weak

NORTHOLME HOTEL
E. Broomhead
Fully licensed

GLACIS, MAHÉ, SEYCHELLES
Three miles from Victoria

Stay with confidence at Northolme.
It enjoys a well-deserved reputation for superb food at its best.
Delightfully situated overlooking the sea, with peaceful background and beautiful scenery.
Private beach.
Goggling, swimming and boating.
24-hour electricity supply.
Hot baths on request daily.

at the knees with hunger and gasping for a drink after our long walk when he finally appeared, made no apology for his tardiness and thereby sowed the first seeds of dissatisfaction on our part with the arrogant attitude of the colonial service. We and the other members of the public had arrived in good time and paid in advance only to be treated with contempt! We might have forgiven him if he had been wearing his funny hat with all the feathers.

Fortunately, Mrs. Broomhead had produced a sumptuous meal that made up for the wait – we waddled off into the darkness with full tummies, longing for our iron bed.

Something we hadn't thought about

But Gill wasn't feeling well. In fact, she hadn't felt well since we were on the ship, not helped every morning by the concerned Indian steward repeatedly asking "No yeggs today, Madam?"

During our short stay at the Beach Hotel we had a chance meeting with Linda, helping out at the hotel reception. Linda, the wife of the ex-government architect and the mother of two small children, had lived in Seychelles for two years. Cheerful, friendly and direct, she was a mine of information concerning buses, or the lack of them, doctors, pharmacies and shops. At her suggestion Gill sat in line outside the outpatients' clinic at the hospital. After a brief examination, elderly and fatherly Dr. Palmer gently enquired "Could you be pregnant, my dear?"

A moment of disorientation, then a picture of a never to be forgotten night on the beach at Xai-Xai, Mozambique in a tent collapsed against the onslaught of swarming mosquitoes. Now we would have another reason to remember that night – though we didn't feel the compulsion to follow a trend and call the baby 'Xai Xai'.

A part of our rebellion against the accepted conventions crumbled at this point. We had never discussed marriage and children except in the context of an already over-populated planet and now we decided that one little baby wasn't going to lead to a population explosion. Also, if we married first and then produced a grandchild, there would be four happy grandparents.

Gisèle, who was the first person we told, was delighted with our news and much to our relief appointed herself organiser of the wedding ceremony. It took place at their now very modest dwelling at Mountain Rise, under the shelter of the Trois Frères mountain range. The official registrar, a skinny Mr. Payet, had pushed his bicycle all the way up the mountain from Victoria to preside over the marriage. Gisèle and Knud were the official witnesses and the only other guests were Klaus, the Alsatian dog, with a large red bow around his neck and little Henry, the maid's son. Knud presented us with an ancient Boxer sword in its original scabbard, so that no man would tear us asunder! The legal papers signed, toasts of wine consumed to the somewhat scratchy strains of 'the Hawaiian Wedding Song' on the record player, Mr. Payet wobbled off on his precipitous bicycle ride back down to Victoria. Our day ended with a steak dinner for four at Northolme hotel – a rare treat on an island where cattle were kept for milk and manure, not meat.

Early next morning we boarded the *Lady Esmé*, the ferry to Praslin island. We didn't realise what the two small towers of plastic bowls at the gangway were for, until we noticed that each Seychelloise lady coming aboard, took a bowl as a necessary precaution against the two hours of wallowing passage that lay ahead of us.

We had been told of a small hotel at Cote d'Or which was run by an English lady, Mrs. Bevan, reputed to be the daughter of Gracie Fields. She was warm and welcoming and pleased to welcome the only two guests to her hotel.

We spent our days taking long walks to the end of Cote d'Or beach and back, never once meeting another soul. The beach of powdery white coral sand held our footprints only until the lazy waves sighed up the beach to wash them away. Under the overhanging palms and lush green Takamaka trees lay a natural hedge of scaevola and mauve flowered carpets of beach morning glory. The small uninhabited Souris Island lay in the wide bay and beyond that, Curieuse island with its red earth showing beneath the scrubby vegetation, witness to fierce fires that once decimated parts of the island.

One day we ventured further afield and visited the Vallée de Mai, home of the legendary coco-de-mer tree – a magical place with an atmosphere of prehistoric times. We followed a narrow gravel path that meandered through the dense palm forest, across a crystal clear stream to a small thatched viewing site. We had the Vallée de Mai to ourselves that day, sharing it with the elusive black parrots conversing in high pitched whistles somewhere in the canopy of wind-ruffled clattering palm fronds. The only other residents were the odd chameleon, large brown geckos, and the brilliant green day geckos with their staring yellow eyes. A small hedgehog-like creature, a tenrec, scuttled away into the undergrowth with a band of stripy babies in tow.

This was the month of the highest rainfall of the year in Seychelles, the north-west monsoon season. And it rained heavily on and off throughout the week. When we were forced to remain indoors, Mrs. Bevan produced an interesting supply of extremely out of date newspapers and magazines from the U.K. We devoured every word!

A second encounter with a property developer

It seemed like a long uphill cycle trip to Vista do Mar each morning, but freewheeling all the way back and meeting Gill at the Goggle and Flipper bar on Beau Vallon beach soon eased me back into a sort of normal life. Derek was an easy going employer and after only two weeks had given me a few days' honeymoon leave and an advance on salary for the purchase of a bicycle.

As the sun went down behind Silhouette island every evening the only person we saw on the beach was Helen, taking a daily evening constitutional walk along the length of the beach, often accompanied by a friendly stray dog, known as 'Pink', in honour of the colour of his nose.

Derek and his Dutch wife, Christina, lived at Fairhaven on the north west of Mahé, not far from Vista do Mar. Fairhaven was an old stone-built palm thatched house, surrounded by extensive gardens. The view from the house was across a small secluded cove and a steep forest- clad landscape beyond. Tucked away in one corner of the property was a small cottage with its feet in the tranquil bay; here, it was rumoured, Ian Fleming had once stayed. Derek was built like 007, good-looking, tanned, muscular, all displayed to full effect by his unique style of dress. He wore a sturdy pair of sandals and a tiny sarong and as was occasionally confirmed when climbing around the building site – no knickers! He was the sort of person it would be impossible to buy a second-hand car from – you were far more likely to be talked into a new Ferrari.

At that stage in its development, Vista do Mar had a very steep surfaced access road and several occupied houses. Setting out and supervising the building of the secondary roads and designing the structural elements of the new houses became my responsibility. Down on the seaside, an old stone-built shop was being rebuilt and extended for use as a restaurant. A footbridge over the road led to the beginnings of a terrace of hotel rooms rising up the steep hillside.

The new inhabitants of Vista do Mar were all well-to-do young English couples, drawn to life in a tropical paradise by Derek's up-market advertising. His cash in hand approach was the reason he was succeeding, unlike the Anse la Mouche development's policy of building by numbers – payment by instalment. He wasn't in any way extravagant other than in his minimal working clothes; he drove a second-hand Austin Champ jeep with a second-hand army truck to transport the building materials. He sometimes donned a safari suit when he needed to impress the bank manager. It wasn't until later in the year when he suddenly cut back on the property development side and could no longer pay salaries that we realised what all those visits to the bank were all about. He did, however, persuade the bank to support the completion of the hotel and restaurant and managed to remain friends with some of the staff he had let down.

Ken's beer money

Our own venture into a very modest property development came about through another chat with Linda during our short stay at the Beach Hotel. She invited us to meet her husband Peter, their two children and the two Labrador dogs. They lived across the road from the hotel, about half a mile from Lyons Corner House. The house had an extensive front garden, consisting of very tall, spindly coconut trees, laden with nuts, and swaying in the breeze. Linda's perpetual warning call to her small daughter as she ran into the garden was to alert her to the potentially lethal danger of "Coconuts!"

On the occasions we were invited to dinner at their home we walked, in the abbreviated equatorial dusk, straight down the middle of the road to Bel Ombre, and never had to give way to any vehicles.

Peter had originally been employed as an architect in the PWD but on completing his two-year contract had taken the opportunity to set up in private practice. His first commission was to design a new building to replace the then falling-apart Pirates Arms Hotel on the Long Pier Road, about a hundred yards from the clock tower in central Victoria. The developer was an ex-bank manager who had invested in several properties on Mahé. Ken also owned Poivre island in the Amirantes group, and a small yacht that meant he did not have to rely on the irregular schooner visits to the islands.

Peter and Linda had bought a plot of land from Ken and were keen to show us the foundations of their dream house – we took the narrow winding road clinging to the mountainside to the far end of Le Niol, across a very narrow wooden bridge spanning a very deep ravine, and on to the short stretch of dirt road, ending up on the steep drive-way that Peter had cut into the sun-baked red earth.

The view from here was spectacular to say the least. The tropical forest tumbled down the steep mountainside, gradually blending in with the coconut plantations and scattered buildings along the shoreline. The mountains on both sides seemed like a wide-armed gesture of wonder at the sweep of Northwest Bay and the blue grey outline of Silhouette island on the distant horizon.

The house was little more than an outline in concrete on the roughly prepared ground. A low wall of several courses of Peter's experimental red-earth and cement bricks was a mere hint of what would soon rise on this mountainside promontory. In retrospect, the house at this stage was at its most orderly. As it grew, it developed into an 'architect's house' with bits and pieces not quite finished or partly changed because of a better idea and allowances made for possible extensions. It was, however, a very creative and cheerful place to be and an adventure house for small children.

As we bumped along the road in the back of Peter's old blue VW beetle, we were more than a little envious of their finding such an incredible spot on the island and of their enthusiastic plans. When we were dropped off at Lyons Corner House, Peter suggested that he could arrange for us to meet Ken as he thought he had other bits of land that he might consider selling. We might have been as poor as two church-mice but our heads were full of dreams.

We met Ken in his new office – the bar at the Beach Hotel, his latest property purchase. When we had expected a stiff, hard-nosed ex-bank manager, we found ourselves being entertained by a rather jovial, friendly person, full of excitement about his new hotel project. Yes, he did in fact have a piece of land that he could find no use for and that might appeal to someone with a small budget and a big imagination.

This, until now, unwanted piece of land was about a mile away from the bar, up two concrete strips set into the red earth track, known as Marie Laure drive. The plot was narrow and wedge-shaped, clamped between the 'road' and a small stream of crystal clear water, murmuring softly as it negotiated its way around the jumble of granite boulders. Some tall sangdragon trees and an old grey-barked cashew tree cast their shade over the huge house-sized boulders with fingers of luxuriant ferns that covered most of the land. The only flat area was the gap between the rocks where the car was parked. We sat on the rocks listening to the sound of the stream and the somnolent cu-cooing of the blue pigeons, wondering if it would be sacrilege to turn this undisturbed morsel of forest into a noisy building site.

Ken came wandering down the road, having ambled off to investigate some activity nearby. "This is where I do my tarty land-dealer bit", he said. "I told you that this wasn't a suitable building site, but if you think you can do something with it, it's yours for £500."

We returned to look at it the following weekend. We wandered about, paddling in the stream, sat on the incredibly large boulders and talked to the blue pigeons. A dapper little sunbird flitted about in the cashew tree, a green day gecko eyeing him suspiciously. After a while even the skinks returned to share with us a sunny spot on the rocks.

The next time we met Ken, we had a vague idea of what we could build. The rules drawn up by the new Führer of the Planning Department dictated the distance to be left between any new building and the road verge. We were also restricted as to how close to the stream we could build. This left us with a space fourteen feet wide which made for an odd-shaped house.

My work with Derek at Vista do Mar had introduced me to the extraordinary skill of the Seychellois masons when it came to building granite walls. We would obviously have ample granite for the walls if we removed the top half of the largest boulder and used the flattened remains as a foundation.

Our main problem, however, was to find the money to buy the land. The best offer we could make was to agree on condition that we could pay it off over several months. Much to our delight Ken was quite pleased with our impecunious offer.

"That'll be fine", he said. "That will keep me in beer money for the next few months."

A puffer fish that looked like Mabel

At this point we had managed to put a few rupees into the bank and were paying Ken's 'beer money' out of the monthly salary from Derek.

'Sex in the palm trees' summed up how some people imagined life in the islands of love. Clearly this was the case for the designer of the 50 Rupee note in cold, distant London.

The prospect of having to find funds to pay the men to blast the top off our gigantic boulder and break it into useable pieces, the masons to build the granite walls and a carpenter to finish off, didn't dampen our spirits. We managed to raise a small loan from one of the two banks on the islands and we were beginning to see an unsteady trickle of income from our still embryonic craftwork.

Tourism in Seychelles in 1970 was totally dependent on the small number of visitors making the sea passage from Mombasa or Bombay on the British India ships. The occasional cruise ship that passed through, stopping for only one or two hours, brought a sudden influx of day visitors to a destination not yet geared up to take large groups on organised tours. Plans were afoot to construct an airport on Mahé as a parting gift from the British government to the inevitable aspirations of independence for the islands.

In our head-in-the-clouds approach, we had not anticipated being somewhat ahead of our time in our artistic endeavours. We had time to study and practise the original batik methods and to work through a range of subjects around the natural history of the islands, especially the gorgeous multi-coloured fish that inhabited the surrounding coral reefs. With the exception of imported dyes, we found all our fabric, candles and beeswax in Market Street or in the market itself.

To begin with, our main outlet was at the Home Industries shop in central Victoria. They supported all local crafts and were pleased to have something entirely new to add to their stock of woodwork, raffia baskets

and place-mats, coconut fibre hats and crochet and smocked dresses. It was through the Home Industries that we received an invitation to go with one or two other craftspeople on board one of the cruise ships.

We were ushered below decks to a corner in one of the lounges, not an obvious place for the passengers to find us. We spread our batik pictures out as best we could and settled down to wait for the rush of wealthy American tourists we assumed made up the bulk of the passengers.

Time passed, a few adventurous people found our corner and looked through the pictures. We must have looked like two under-nourished hippies with the prospect of a visit to the maternity ward looming in the not too distant future. Two large, obviously well-fed American ladies wandered over and were being very friendly and complimentary when one of them suddenly yelled in excitement, "My gaad, Susan, will ya look at this! I really gotta have it – it looks just like Mabel!" She was waving one of the batiks depicting a puffer fish with its swollen belly and protruding buggy teeth. Poor Mabel, she probably never heard the end of it – puffer fish aren't the prettiest fish in the sea.

Every little success like this helped to boost our belief that we would one day survive on our craftwork alone, but with pie-in-the-sky plans to build a house and replace the bicycle age with something that could transport two and a half people, anything that brought in extra money was a penny from heaven. Fortunately, a well-used palette, brushes and several tubes of oil paint had been squeezed into our packing from South Africa, so that when Knud commissioned an oil painting for a restaurant he was designing and building, we were happy to oblige.

Seychelles first gourmet restaurant

The 'Refuge du Corsaire' restaurant was being built on the foundations of an old shop right on the edge of the sea, adjacent to the moorings used by all the Bel Ombre fishermen. When complete, it was a single storey, half-timbered, heavily thatched building, with interior décor that fulfilled its atmospheric name.

We found an old piece of canvas sail cloth which Knud had his carpenters stretch onto a wooden frame. We sized that canvas as best we could and set about depicting a legendary eighteenth century Anglo-French sea battle. We found in someone's shed, a rusty tin of once-used varnish with which to coat the painting, giving it a slight yellow-with-age look. It was finally removed from the stretcher to ensure a few cracks in the varnish. Reframed in an old recycled frame, the painting was hung as a feature in the restaurant.

Knud and Gisèle were both heavily involved in the interior design of the restaurant and dealing with the demands and desires of the Belgian couple who were to run it. Gisèle, with her Belgian roots, was keen for us to get to know M. et Mme. William, who were obviously more fussed about how the kitchen was arranged and about the quality of the cutlery and crockery, rather than the decor.

When the Refuge du Corsaire opened, M. William was the chef for a few weeks but then quite suddenly packed up and disappeared. Mme. William accepted the challenge of managing what was the first real top-class restaurant in the islands. The cost of meals was beyond our meagre means, but fortunately we two waifs from Lyons Corner House had the occasional meal at the Corsaire when we swapped processed Kraft cheese for real Camembert and enjoyed good company as guests of Gisèle and Knud.

Sleepless nights at Sans Soucis

Gisèle had decided that our humble abode, tucked away at it was in the undergrowth on the coastal plateau, was not a healthy, comfortable environment for Gill's developing pregnancy – especially during the doldrum period; those sweaty airless months between the monsoon and the tradewinds. She had heard that the government vet and his wife were about to depart on extended overseas leave and were looking for someone to house-sit during their absence. Their house was perched high on the mountainside overlooking Victoria and the cluster of small islands that protected the anchorage. It was also within walking distance of Mountain Rise where Gisèle and Knud lived.

It was much cooler up there, especially with the first stirring of the south east trade-wind. And, Oh! What bliss – a bed with a proper mattress instead of the iron frame and lumpy coir mattress we were used to. There was also a properly equipped kitchen with a real fridge and a cooker, a comfy sofa instead of deckchairs and even a telephone that meant we no longer had to make the journey to Cable and Wireless where the only two public phones were located. To complete the picture of homely comforts were Ethel, the dog, and Jonathan, the ginger tomcat.

The improvement in our living conditions now that we didn't have to listen to Jim Reeves any longer, also gave us the quiet time we needed to decide what name to give to our imminent offspring. We decided that if it was a girl we would call her Anna, and we'd call a boy either Karl or better still, a French-sounding name like Justin, in honour of bilingual Seychelles. That nail-biting day was upon us in mid-July when Gill started feeling uncomfortable followed by cramps in the tum. This first encounter with birth pangs turned out to be just a practice run and had to be repeated in earnest later in the month. In view of this, Justin's maternal grandfather could not resist the quip "Justin time!" when he eventually arrived.

As this memorable day progressed, we slowly positioned ourselves closer to the hospital in case of emergency. A leisurely fish and chip lunch at Rocco's opposite failed to speed things up and it wasn't until the evening when we dared to present ourselves again – this time it must be for real! A long night followed with great cooperation from the team of midwives and Dr. Rick who had become a friend over the previous months with me nervously present until Gill was wheeled to the delivery room. Then, bleary-eyed and dishevelled, as the sun came up over the eastern horizon, I received the news from Rick that Sunday morning 26th July, that Justin had made his appearance.

We didn't realise, when we left the hospital a few days later with our new baby, that we would soon think that Jim Reeves would have been preferable to the endless, sleepless nights that followed. One morning, three months later, we woke to find sunshine streaming through the window and not a sound from the cot. The first time in three months! In sheer panic we rushed to see if something awful had happened, only to find a happy, smiling Justin having also enjoyed his first proper full night's sleep. We never again had to put him in the back of the car and drive around until he fell asleep.

In this new luxurious abode we felt that our stars were coming together. Not only did we have a new baby, we had also acquired a car. It was a necessary evil, as a bicycle ride to work at Vista do Mar would have taken half a day each way, leaving only enough time to eat an exhausted lunch and no time to work. The car was Peter's old battered blue VW beetle. He had bought a brand new mini minibus which seemed barely big enough to accommodate his family. We were given first option on the beetle but obviously didn't have the cash. This problem was resolved on a like-for-like basis. If I would like to design the structure for Peter's newest architectural project, the major extension to Richard's supermarket Peter would like to give me his VW in return – no money involved.

This new found mobility came in handy when we started clearing our piece of land in preparation for the blasting and breaking up of our biggest boulder. The house at Sans Soucis had given us an idea as to how we could design a building to fit on our oddly-shaped boulder- strewn plot. We decided that we could use our ample supply of granite to construct two parallel walls, twenty feet apart. In this enclosed space would be the sitting room with glass doors opening onto a wooden deck that would give us a view of the sea through the overhanging branches of the old cashew tree. More glass doors would open onto a small level area between the boulders overlooking the jungle-shrouded stream. The kitchen, dining area and bathroom would be at this level. A part-granite, part-wooden staircase led to a small bedroom suitable for a forthcoming family member, and to the main bedroom galleried over the sitting room, affording free movement of air and mosquitoes through the building. Later, we were fortunate to find a large heap of unbroken mangalore roof tiles from a demolished building, sufficient to cover the roof.

This design was given planning permission and whenever we sold a few batiks or raided the housekeeping money, we were able to employ some of the men from Vista do Mar, at weekends or after work, to start the building work.

Sleeping with centipedes

Work on our house was progressing well, thanks to a loan from the bank and a reliable team of builders. It was, however, not remotely habitable when our house-sitting at Sans Soucis came to an end and it looked as though we would be homeless for a while. We were rescued by Madame William who offered us a room in her small corrugated iron house on the beach, not far from the Corsaire. Not only did she offer us somewhere to live, she would often wake us late at night with a dish or two of Corsaire kitchen leftovers like boeuf bourgignon or chocolate mousse! If she was not too busy at the restaurant, she sometimes invited us over for a meal and even sent Virginie, one of her staff, to babysit while we were out.

One evening, accepting her invitation, we ambled over to the Corsaire and found Derek and Christina treating themselves to a great indulgence. We were more than a little upset, having been told by Derek that morning that he was in financial difficulties and could no longer pay salaries, and yet here he was in the most expensive restaurant having a multi-course meal with expensive French wine to boot! His financial difficulties, that were obviously not personal, demanded a rethink of his priorities and led to his closing down the property side of his business and concentrating on the restaurant and hotel projects. This was when I found myself once more in full-time unemployment. In a way it came as a blessing; I was able to devote all my time to getting the house built and designing the basic furniture we needed.

There was more to living in Mme. William's house than the wonderful meals. The beach was a mere twenty feet from the door and we were able to treat Justin to his first introduction to the warm Indian Ocean. Had he experienced the close encounters with the local wildlife that we had at this time, he might not have grown up with a fascination for those things that sting and bite.

In the early hours of the morning, before the equatorial sun comes rushing over the horizon, when sleep is sometimes most profound, the world is supposed to be at its most peaceful. On such a morning, Gill suddenly leapt out of bed, shouting and grabbing at her leg. A searing pain like having a burning coal thrust into her flesh made us both abandon ship and set about ripping the sheet from the bed to expose a six inch long centipede scuttling over the edge and onto the floor. We moved all the furniture around until we found it and took our revenge. We thought that such things happened only once, but we were to learn that centipedes enjoy the damp warmth of human bodies, but object like mad when the bodies move. After a few days, the swelling and the persistent ache disappear, but not the fear of centipedes – the most dangerous creature in Seychelles.

Towards the end of the year, we exchanged the sound of the monsoon rain thundering down on Madame's tin roof for the roaring river that our quiet little stream had become. But, we were hearing it from the luxury of our own bed in our own house. When it wasn't raining, the sun sparkled on the leaves, the river subsided into its idyllic stream-like self and the barred ground doves kept up their early morning conversations as they looked for seeds among the rocks.

It seemed that we had acquired a baby, house and car – all the important elements of the life we had so recently rejected. We did still have the dream of being able to live our own self-sufficient lives, but that was something for the future.

Tourism was the colonial government's solution to making the islands' economy viable. Many of Britain's colonial possessions on tropical islands had relied on inadequate economies based on vegetable oil produced from vast coconut plantations, or as in the case of Seychelles, the trade in cinnamon bark. The planned airport and the increase in the number of tourists was seen as the way forward. We all thought this was a jolly good idea and wished they would hurry up and finish the runway.

Chapter 3

<u>A close encounter with a spook</u>
The first few months in our new home were absolute bliss. It wasn't quite finished because there was no sheet glass available on the island and we had to wait for a ship to bring new supplies. In the interim we used plastic sheeting fixed into all of our 'glass doors'. This gave a somewhat impressionistic view of the garden and a strange eerie breathing sound at night when the wind blew through the house.

One morning, shortly after we had been blessed with a telephone line, we had a call from Madame William asking us to stop by at the Corsaire. On the way down the road, the old VW's steering felt a bit sluggish – a reminder that the months of hauling bags of cement up to the building site had taken their toll. We weren't away from the car for more than half an hour, but in that time our hardworking little vehicle had had a major suspension attack and had subsided onto its nose, front wheels leaning out alarmingly. A frantic phone call brought Ernestine and his breakdown truck to the rescue.

Truth to tell though, the beetle had seen better days and in any case, where on an island a thousand miles from anywhere would we find the necessary spare parts?

Ernestine had recently completed an exhaustive overhaul of a charming-looking VW Karmann Ghia – a sort of poor man's Porsche. We made a deal with him, trading in our wreck for what turned out to be his load of trouble. She really didn't like the humidity and often needed a hefty kick in the tyres to persuade her to move.

She only had two doors, so it came as a nasty surprise when one day, as we were making our way up the steep winding road towards St. Louis, one of those two doors decided to swing open of its own volition. Coming down the hill; two wheels on the central white line, a big shiny newish car received a blood-chilling metallic swipe from our pale grey door. The driver and his intimidating wife with bottom lip and self-important bust jutting out like shelves piled out of their car and looked at the newly embellished grey stripe along the length of it.

Horrors! We recognised him as someone who had something to do with the police. He started shouting. Embarrassed, apologetically we tried to

pacify him.
"Do you know who I am?" he yelled.
"Yes. Sorry. You are from the police. Sorry."
"No, I am not. I am head of security."
"Sorry."
"All the islands need is a pair of hippies like you."
Strange, we hadn't thought of ourselves with flowers in our hair, we thought we were more smoky coffee shop and jazz people.
"Sorry. It was an accident. Sorry"
"You will pay for this. I'll have you off the island before you can draw breath." His self-important apoplexy rose like a scarlet tide, spreading across his face and blocking his ears.

We should have told him to clear off, but that would have reinforced his preconception that we were the unwashed unemployed. It was sheer good fortune that several months earlier, when I had stopped working for Derek, the immigration department had insisted that it was necessary to obtain a self-employed work permit. This, and a good character reference from one of Gisèle's friends – the chief of police – put an end to the threat of revenge. All we had to do was pay for the repairs – fortunately the grey streak was easy to remove, probably the result of Ernestine having painted the Karmann Ghia with something like emulsion paint.

Little did we know that some years later we would be treated to the picture, on BBC TV, of this security bully being interviewed back home in U.K., having been 'thrown off the island' by the post independence revolutionary government of 1977.

It was the beginning of the end for Karmann; she was suffering from the humidity – a sort of car asthma. Karmann's failing health, coupled with our scepticism about Ernestine's mechanical skills, prompted us to make frequent stops at a makeshift garage at the top of the hill above Beau Vallon. George, in his greasy overalls, was typical of all motor mechanics on the islands, home-grown backyard experts who filled a vital need for owners of ageing vehicles. The last time we saw Karmann before she joined the row of rusting wrecks at George's shambolic garage, she was straddled over the garage pit and a grease-covered mechanic was sitting in the dust, entangled in yards of copper wire from her dynamo. Her replacement was Japanese, bought from Kim Koon's Chinese emporium; the funds coming from a commission for a sculpture for the new Pirates Arms hotel.

Still somewhat aggrieved by the threats from the security man, I chose a political theme for the sculpture. There were to be three adjoining panels to the left of the entrance to the hotel; each about ten feet wide by eight feet high. The 'sculpture', if concrete panels could be called sculpture, was to take the form of multiple adjoining triangles. The left panel was to represent the slaves – a crowd of downward pointing triangles. The centre panel; more horizontal triangles, suggesting hooded eyes and pith helmet, was to be the governor and the right panel with triangles radiating from a central point, the angry eyes and fist of the rebel. Later, when the hotel opened and its spacious restaurant and coffee shop became the most popular meeting place in Victoria, the abstract panels were merely part of the modern architecture – but I felt a lot better.

When the initial drawings for the sculpture had been completed, we took a run up to Peter and Linda's house at Le Niol to discuss the practicalities of making the panels. Looking at the view as we were getting ready to leave, we saw two men walking along a newly cut road on the hillside below.

"Those are my clocktower girls"

The airport was beginning to be a reality in early 1971; land had been reclaimed from the sea at Pointe Larue and concrete was being laid on the runway. The Reef Hotel, the first of the modern beach hotels that would replace the small local hotels with their homely atmosphere, was under construction. There was a wave of excitement and optimism about these changes and the future of tourism on the island.

We had met the two men we had seen on the road below Peter and Linda's house. They were yet another pair of property developers seeking to make their fortune by building a hotel and at the same time getting permission to build luxury housing for foreigners. Because of the foreign investment it engendered, this lucrative private housing development was given government approval.

They were looking for someone with engineering experience to organise and manage the building of their hotel, without the need to employ a registered building contractor. At the same time they wanted to start building the houses at Casuarina Hills which is what they called the development on the mountainside where we had seen them.

The site for the Coral Strand Hotel was on Beau Vallon beach, the safest and most beautiful beach in Seychelles, with its fringe of dense shady Takamaka trees. We were told from the outset that this was going to be the first five star hotel on the islands. The three storey building was to be of the highest standard, no expense spared and had to be completed in eighteen months. General management of the project and seeing that the right bits of reinforcing bars went into the right bits of concrete were

46

to be my responsibility while the task of supervising the tradesmen and the quality of their work fell to John – someone with years of experience on building sites in the UK and a stickler for detail.

The structure actually went up in a relatively short time, but the finishes were to take much longer, especially with John's drive for perfection. What we were most proud of was not so much the quality of the work, but that our team, some two hundred strong at one point, were all Seychellois.

As the building grew out of the sand on the edge of the sea, it began to attract attention. We had several impromptu visits from the Chief Minister of the Legislative Assembly, clad only in his swim suit. Later, as work progressed, there were protocol-led visits from Archbishop Makarios and his black-gowned entourage during his brief visit to the islands of his earlier exile. This time, instead of being sent to the islands as a prisoner of the British colonial administration, he visited freely as president of independent Cyprus.

During the official visit to Seychelles by Princess Margaret and Anthony Armstrong-Jones, their tour of the island included a scheduled stop at Beau Vallon for the princess to admire our most beautiful beach. Protocol must have decided that her husband would prefer something more masculine, like a visit to our nearby building site. As a special treat during his visit we were able to offer him a ride to the dizzy heights of the second floor of the Coral Strand in the first and only lift on the islands. He seemed suitably impressed with the honour.

The most memorable visit, though, was not a celebrity at all. One afternoon a strange silence fell over the site – these were the 'old days' when building sites were totally male-dominated – there was a communal sigh and a surreptitious shuffling to get a better look at the tall, strikingly beautiful blonde who had just come out of the sea looking for all the world like Ursula Andress in 'Dr. No'. She was trailing an elegant young man behind her and made her way to our office. There was a scramble to see who could get there first to find out why the couple were lost.

Guye, or Gaia as we called her, introduced herself and her husband Joe, and asked if we could help them out with a loan of a few bags of cement for the house they were renovating nearby. I would willingly have lent her a whole truck load of this sometimes scarce resource. There was a bit of a tussle between the two people allowed to drive the pick-up, Johnny and Juan, but in the end Johnny delivered the cement.

The pick-up was handy at times when it wasn't busy and it could be despatched to Bel Ombre to collect Gill and Justin and bring them to the beach. It was the perfect place for mothers with small children who met there in the afternoon under the shade of the Takamaka trees. Beau Vallon beach, sheltered from the trade-wind where the warm sea near the shore was calm and safe even for toddlers.

Sometimes on a Saturday afternoon, if work wasn't too pressing, I joined the beachgoers under the trees and often Dr. Rick and his wife and their kids were there too. On some of those lazy afternoons, three or four buxom young women, sporting Indian-made pointy bras in lieu of bikini tops, would pass, waving and making friendly signs to Rick.

Barbara would raise an eyebrow.

"Friends of yours? she'd ask Rick.

"They're some of my clock-tower girls. Regulars at my clap clinic", he'd say with a wry smile.

The clock-tower girls were part of the old reputation that Seychelles were the islands of love. On the ship on my very first trip to the islands there had been two South African men in their sixties who made the journey to find love, because they had heard that in Seychelles 'fish were were ten for a shilling and girls were ten for a fish'. Unfortunately for these men, although I heard a lot of snuffling and girlish giggling coming from one of their rooms adjacent to mine in the so-called beach apartments of the Hotel des Seychelles, the other rooms were rented for the same assignations by lusty American from the U.S. tracking station that sat like two huge golf balls on the mountain above La Misère. These were all single young men with incomes that seemed like small fortunes to anyone else working on the islands.

What we liked about the Americans was not so much the economic benefit to the clock-tower girls, but their Catalina flying boat that landed with a roar and clouds of spray as it taxied in the sea alongside Long Pier Road every Thursday. The Catalina brought all the airmail post which it had collected in Mombasa. The mail bags were delivered to the post office, where the staff immediately set about sorting the letters and stuffing them into the post office boxes. We, the public, who were expecting mail, having watched the sea-plane arrive, retreated to 'The Rainbow'. This was a bar about twenty-five yards from the Post Office, upstairs in the Mahé Trading building. We had about an hour to kill which gave ample time to socialise, to catch up with Gisèle and others on the previous week's goings on and the island gossip. It was a friendly but rowdy interlude which lasted until we got the signal that the mail was sorted.

There was a moment of quiet in the Rainbow as night descended on the island. Then the Americans, their hangers-on and the girls from the clock-tower drifted in, making much more noise than the post office crowd and probably spent ten times more at the bar.

It was all about to change. The Catalina's weekly visits were replaced by a regular light aircraft service that could use the soon to be completed airport runway. The post office gave up its quaint habit of sorting mail on the spot and made us wait until the next day. The Rainbow was not immune to the change; customers began to favour the newly opened pavement level café and bar at the Pirates Arms as a place to meet friends and be seen.

The big change for the Rainbow however, was something that took everyone by surprise. Gaia and Joe saw the decline in customers as a golden opportunity to do something different for the night life of Victoria. As the colours of the Rainbow faded, so they were replaced by the dimmed ambience and disco music of La Gigolette, the first night club in Seychelles.

Birds of passage

A vast crowd of inquisitive, excited onlookers had gathered at the airport to witness the arrival of the first ever tourist flight into Seychelles. It was July 1971, and while most people were familiar with the old Catalina flying boat, very few indeed had ever seen and heard what to them was the unimaginable size and noise of a VC10 aircraft thundering and screaming its way down the runway. The first familiar face to disembark was Jimmy, our flamboyant Chief Minister, in his best suit and tie, waving to the crowd with an almost theatrical flourish. This was the same Chief Minister who used to inspect the building of the Coral Strand in his swimming trunks. Most of the crowd though were far more interested in the latest clothes being worn by the ladies filing down the gangway like models on a catwalk. This flutter of tourists in their finery brought to mind the flocks of migrating birds taking refuge from the northern winter in the warmth on the tidal flats alongside Long Pier Road.

These new birds of passage on the runway were the first sign that tourism had finally arrived; the British government must have heaved a sigh of relief as it looked as though tourists promised to replace cinnamon and coconuts as the mainstay of the economy of these soon to be independent islands.

Tourism had definitely not taken off at the Coral Strand. Towards the end of the year, despite all the frantic efforts, a sense of panic prevailed. John was pulling his hair out as we saw the quality of the imported furnishings fall well below the standard of the building.

It was all part of the money-saving compromise we had been promised would not happen. As we struggled to finish the massive wooden structure of the two storey restaurant, we were confronted by the arrival of the future manager and the head chef, both of whom wanted things moved and rearranged to suit their needs. All this and the news that the first guests were booked in for the New Year and there was not the slightest prospect of the hotel being fully ready.

Fortunately, the chaos at work did not extend as far as home, except for those evenings when we were invited out for a meal and, through sheer exhaustion, I started snoring in the middle of the dessert. We were glad of the distraction from work day problems when Gill's mum decided to come out to meet her grandson. Grandma, as she was known from then on, arrived on one of the first flights.

We managed to rearrange our house, designed for two and a bit people, into a two bedroomed house by squeezing a bed into 'Justin's room' and found space for his cot in our room. Grandma politely accepted this somewhat cramped arrangement and was happy to get to know her first grandchild. One morning she came down to breakfast, looking rather flustered.

"I felt something walking on my legs during the night. I didn't want to disturb you" she said.

"Perhaps it was a gecko, fallen off the ceiling?"

She shook her head "No. Bigger – with feet – walking".

We couldn't bring ourselves to tell her that 'bigger', 'feet', 'walking', spelt rat!

We went to Adam Moosa's shop and bought one of those walk-in traps, not really thinking about what to do with a live rat in a trap.. But Grandma had proved herself braver than a friend's mother, who, taking a sip from a glass of water during the night, just avoided a mouthful of gecko as it swam valiantly around and around in her glass. This horrified lady rushed to the airport as soon as she could the next morning to catch the first flight back to civilisation, never to return.

George Bibi came to the rescue. Some months previously he had stood on the roadside, shouting "Madame – Madame" to attract attention, as people do in Seychelles. He had come to offer his services as our gardener and had such a polite, friendly manner that we gave him the job there and then, despite his having only one arm. He had lost the other arm at an early age when a coconut fell on it, damaging it so badly that it had to be amputated. He was an amazing person: even with only one arm, George was capable of scrambling over the huge boulders where he used a primitive version of hydroponics to grow vegetables for us. He made 'kapatya' – woven palm-frond baskets which he stacked on the top of the boulders, filled them with compost he had made and kept them well-watered.

He always had time to chat to Justin when he was out in his pram, and later when he could walk, showing him things of interest that he found in the garden. He took the cage with Grandma's rat inside and came back ten minutes later with the trap re-set with a lump of coconut as bait – Seychelles rats didn't understand that cheese was edible.

Some days when the pick-up, or Johnny, or both, were too busy to collect Gill, Grandma and Justin to bring them to the beach, they trundled down the bumpy road to visit a friend who lived at the bottom of the hill. These trips involved guiding the pushchair with its complaining squeaky wheels past the home of the Master of the local Masonic Lodge. He never missed the chance to rush out onto the road with his oil can to ease the painful squeaking - or maybe it was just the chance to have a chat with a pretty young girl and her mum. The oil never seemed to solve the squeaking and he never missed a chance to show his concern.

One important date when I knew they couldn't be left at home was during Princess Margaret's visit to Seychelles when she was scheduled to make a brief stop to see the beach at Beau Vallon. This was the same stop on her tour of the island that brought Tony Armstrong Jones to the Coral Strand and allowed us to give him that exciting experience - a ride in the island's first lift.

I made sure that Johnny collected Gill, Grandma and Justin well ahead of time so that they could join what we expected would be Princess Margaret's welcoming crowd on the beach.

It was hardly a crowd, more like a somewhat rag-tag bunch of people confused by the arrival of a vehicle on the beach and a rather short princess alighting onto the sand. It was as though they had been expecting someone so important to be ten feet tall and wearing a crown. If our Chief Minister had been royalty, he would have worn a crown everywhere he went, but here was a princess and she didn't even have a hat!

Grandma poked Gill in the ribs.

"Do you think we should cheer?"

The crowd watched the princess in silence.

"Sing God Save the Queen?" she suggested, sotto voce. The silence seemed to last an eternity

"Oh, come on - let's do something!"

That seemed to break the spell and a few gentle claps joined Grandma's thunderous applause.

Princess Margaret, who had taken in the scenery, returned to the vehicle, took off her shoes, banged them against the car to dislodge the sand, and was driven away. The onlookers resumed their daily routines, a couple of fishermen wandered back to their nets, ladies picked up their bundles of mackerel and headed off home. Gill and Grandma found a shady place where they waited for Johnny and the pick-up to collect them after their exciting afternoon.

Grandma was still ensconced in Justin's room, enjoying the days sunbathing on the beach or sitting quietly with her knitting under the trees at the house, when two small birds of passage arrived from South Africa. My father's elder sister, Heidi and her husband Harry, were both only about five feet tall but made up for their lack of altitude by being loud and jovial. They were booked in at Tante Mimi's Sunset Hotel - a few detached bungalows and an unremarkable building serving as reception, bar and restaurant. The hotel sat on a rocky cape where the sea surged restlessly between the rocks and made its way onto a small sheltered beach. Unlike the gardens at nearby Northolme, here the ground was raked and swept clean in true island fashion. Mimi was about the same height as Heidi and Harry and ran a tight ship, expecting guests to obey rules and meal times.

We wanted to take all the family on a tour around the island, but needed something larger than our car - the back seat of which barely accommodated Grandma and Justin. The Coral Strand pick-up seemed to be the only available alternative but would mean some-one - or two - sitting in the open air in the back.

And so, on a bright sunny day we set off from Sunset with Harry and me in the cab and Heidi, Gill and Grandma enthroned like royalty in two of Tante Mimi's armchairs in the back, looking after Justin in his baby recliner at their feet.

The pedestrians plodding along the road were greeted with regal waving, or peals of laughter whenever the chairs slid about as we negotiated the tight bends of the winding roads. We stopped high in the mountains to look at the view, but had to leave the ladies in their armchairs where they were more comfortable then they would have been climbing down over the truck's tailgate. The coastal road almost circumnavigated the island, past the sandy bays shaded by palms interspersed with dramatic stretches of weather and wave-beaten sculptured rocks. In places the road turned inland, winding through the mountains. The unsteady perches in the back of the truck gave the best of the fantastic views through dense forest to the ridges below the towering granite mountain peaks. There were also glimpses through the trees of the endless Indian Ocean, curving away on the horizon, or, at some points, views of the other islands. Our visitors could hardly fail to be impressed by this overwhelmingly beautiful island.

It wasn't long after our visitors left that Gill had to make her own passage north to attend her brother Steve's wedding. She would have to cope alone with the joys of air travel with a 20-month old Justin as I was needed at work, especially now that the Coral Strand was looking more like a hotel than a bomb site; there was even the beginnings of a swimming pool. The insubstantial barrier of beach sand that kept the sea at bay was no protection at high tide when the water percolated through the sand and tried to flood the excavation. Two borrowed pumps struggled valiantly to keep the hole dry, or to empty it each time the tide flooded into the swimming pool.

Chapter 4

<u>A brief trip to the smoke</u>
Gill's brother Steve's marriage to Stephanie took place in March 1972. Arriving at Heathrow airport in a still wintery England, Justin was installed on top of the luggage trolley and wheeled out of the airport building into the cold. It was his first experience of an air temperature less than 25° celsius.

"Look, smoke!" he cried, as his first breath hit the cold, "Smoke". Another puff, more 'smoke'. He must have wondered how he could suddenly blow smoke like many adults could do, but he didn't even need a cigarette.

The happy wedding day arrived, providing an opportunity for Gill to catch up with her relations and for them to meet this new member of the family. During the pause for photographs outside the church, one of the bride's uncles sidled up to Gill and said he had visited Seychelles while on active service during the war. He gave a deep sigh, as though remembering the beauty of the islands.

"Are the girls still so very friendly?" he asked.

Two weeks later it was time to catch the plane home and only then did Justin finally get his biological clock sorted out and stopped wanting to get out of bed and play at four in the morning, every day. Left to my own devices during Gill's absence, I was happy to be invited out for a meal with Mme. William at the Corsaire; this gourmet experience came as a welcome change from the rather mundane meals of my limited repertoire. Gisèle also fed me on a couple of evenings. Knud had been at a bit of a loose end since the completion of the Corsaire and had had to sell the property at Cap Soleil at North-east point, to keep them going. In his new found freedom, now that he no longer had to keep office hours, he immersed himself in astrology, trying to convince himself that there was a scientific basis for the influence the planets were thought to have on human behaviour. He also took to drinking four or five beers at lunchtime and in the evening would join Gisèle and me as we demolished a bottle or two of Mateus Rosé or an acidic South African plonk imported by Temooljee's Indian grocery store. When Gisèle wasn't listening, we referred to it as Chateau Temooljee.

On a corner in the middle of town there was a tiny statue of Queen Victoria. She seemed to have her disapproving gaze fixed on the lopsided weather vane on top of the clock-tower, which is maybe why she looked so severe. Queen Elizabeth was, however, a constant image in everyone's mind and her portrait hung in every government office, the bank and the post office. Portraits of the Queen and other royal family members cut out of newspapers decorated the walls of many humble homes.

Queen Victoria had her back to Fiennes Esplanade which was the grandiose name given to the pavement that ran along the shoreline to Le Chantier. About halfway along the esplanade a dirt track called the Short Pier extended out to the yacht club and facing tiny Hodoul island. We were not members of the yacht club but had the occasional drink there with Knud and Gisèle as well as sometimes attending a good film show.

On the short pier road, almost blocking the way, stood a large wooden schooner hull, propped up on timber fence posts. Below the plimsoll line was a scattering of wooden plugs, jutting out like the spines on a sea urchin. Its presence was annoying the yacht club members but not nearly as much as it upset the port authorities. Every time they demanded that the boat be refloated and taken away, the owner, Harvey, an anorexic little man in vast baggy khaki shorts, his legs hanging out like sticks, would find another probable leak in the hull and drive another wooden plug into it. Although he probably knew the hull was slowly rotting away, he insisted on his right to make his boat seaworthy before launching it. In the meantime it stood there like a monument to the age of trading schooners and Harvey had made his own political statement to the port authorities. He was soon to lose his battle when he had to make way for progress as the Victoria shoreline was about to change forever. The Yacht Club would no longer be isolated on the end of the short pier road, it would be on the sea-front on land reclaimed from the sea. To make room for an expanding Victoria this reclamation engulfed the long pier road

56

and all the tidal flats, taking with them Harvey's boat.

The Queen and Prince Philip paid an official visit to Seychelles that year, despite the beginnings of serious political unrest that had come to the fore in February. The two main political parties were taking diametrically opposite stands on the future of the islands. The Chief Minister and his chums supported the colonial government's view that future economic security would best be found in tourism and he and his party wanted to remain under the protection of the British crown.

The opposition would have none of this. They said tourism would further enslave the people, forcing them into a life of servitude as cleaners and waiters and that nothing short of full independence from Britain was acceptable. To show how determined and serious their demands were, they exploded bombs at the Reef Hotel and at Adam Moosa's shop in Victoria. No-one was hurt, but a point had been made.

The Queen's visit went ahead as scheduled and large crowds of happy people lined the streets to wave and cheer. Her portrait was to adorn all the public offices for another four years. Queen Victoria would, however, carry on scowling at the clock-tower until she was moved to a new location where she could keep an eye on the comings and goings across the road at the Post Office. This might have been a bit more interesting than the weather-vane, but it never seemed to make her any happier.

A studio to call our own

One weekend George the gardener and I built a carport and a studio in the garden with some materials I had scrounged from work. We laid a concrete floor between two of our gigantic boulders and made a roof of timber beams and clear plastic roof sheeting which ensured maximum light in the dappled shade of the overhanging trees.

It was a good place for George to store his tools but its more important function was to stop me from making an inconvenient mess in the kitchen when Gill was trying to cook, and the acrid smell of the molten wax used in the batik process could be banished to this airy studio to be shared with the wildlife – actually the bees found the smell of molten beeswax very enticing.

The bright natural light, the sound of the stream running between the rocks and the gentle conversation of the barred ground doves made this little studio the perfect place to work. It was my very first purpose-built studio and it brought to mind how, as a child I used to sit in the evening at the kitchen table copying in great detail illustrations from the cowboy stories my father read. Mom was there too, smocking babies' dresses while we listened to Inspector West or 'The Saint' on the radio. At high school art was not considered a subject serious enough to be included in the final years of study, but later I was given an easel and painted and drew in my bedroom.

My parents too, like all good parents, did not cherish the thought of my wanting to be an artist; they thought that artists starved in their cobweb-draped garrets or had to cut off an ear like Vincent to attract attention – a very prescient idea really. A cut-off ear floating in a glass of gin and tonic would probably win the Turner Prize in our shock-art era.

So it came as a surprise when despite this lack of formal training, here in Seychelles I was asked to join the local art group organised and run by the government architect and his wife. The aim of the group was to set up an informal art school to encourage young Seychellois to develop their artistic talents. There was an old building used as a school meals centre adjacent to the bus terminus which had two spacious rooms free. We named it Camion Hall in honour of the buses - those temporarily converted lorries called 'camions' The Camion Hall Art School, workshop and gallery opened its doors to its first group of students who were mostly bored expat wives, but fortunately included a few bright young Seychellois. Classes were held in the evenings but the gallery, which was run on a voluntary basis, was intended for specific exhibitions.

While Camion Hall provided us with a limited outlet for our craftwork, Gill and I benefitted most from sales at the Home Industries shop which was tucked in between the Magistrates Court and Barclays Bank and was run by the lovely, motherly Mme. Tirant. Shortly after Gill's return from the wedding in England, Mme. Tirant invited us to participate in the Festival of Art and Crafts exhibition, which in turn opened up

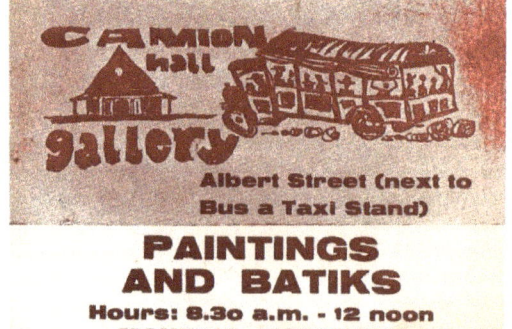

other possibilities for us.

We were asked to exhibit several batik paintings in the restaurant at Vista do Mar which was managed by Frankie, who owned a house on the estate next to the hotel. The trick for us was to ensure we always had a replacement ready to fill the gap when there was a sale. Under the circumstances of the pressing need to complete the contract at the Coral Strand, batik production had to be squeezed into late nights and spare moments.

As the year progressed and the developers' idea of a deadline for the opening of the Coral Strand drew nearer, John and I struggled with the problems caused by the late ordering and shipment of materials and furnishings.

John was particularly offended by the rounded tops to the prefabricated wardrobes that we had to fit into rooms of straight horizontal and vertical lines.

"They look like a pair of elephant bums", he despaired.

"We have no choice, John, we have to get this finished. Just think, you'll never have to look at them again after the opening!"

"Humff. Bugger it", he offered, and stalked off.

This was nothing compared to our comments about the hotel logo we later had to place on the canopy over the reception area. It was supposed to represent a conch shell but to our jaded eyes, it looked more like something the dog had left behind.

A team of Mauritians was rushed in to lay terrazzo in all the rooms and along the corridors, a slow and messy business that sent a watery sludge from the surface grinders trickling down into the rooms below. There was a sewage treatment plant to commission and a quarter of a mile long pipe to install, in order to discharge the treated effluent out to sea. The electrics, plumbing, air conditioning, painting and decorating and to cap it all, this strange restaurant building with its heavy timber columns to construct – all had to be completed before New Year.

The early arrival of the manager and head chef added to our woes. They wanted things rearranged at the last minute, changes made, priorities rescheduled and the kitchen almost redesigned.

There was a moment of relief when the chef needed to know what we locals thought of the islands' various exotic tropical fruits. The hotel was obviously going to make far greater demands on the local fruit than we could imagine, but we had a few ideas of what his guests might like and some they definitely wouldn't even want to try.

Breadfruit, those hard, cannon ball-sized fruits, made excellent chips but came in seasonal gluts, as did the various breeds of mango. The local oranges were a total disaster as they had more pips than flesh. The varieties of banana were superb, with thin skins and delicate flavours. Papaya, or paw-paw as we called it, depended not only on the variety but on where and how it was grown. They could be sweet and tasty but occasionally could taste – as the French author Louis Ferdinand Céline put it – "like pissed-on pear".

The strangest looking fruit was jakfruit, a huge bag of rough green skin that clung to the trunk of its parent tree. It contained many seeds encased in a tasty flesh – the problem being the cat's pee smell. If you managed to get the fruit past your nose, the taste was unique.

Another problem fruit, but probably not one that would ever be served at the Coral Strand, was santol – a sort of furry yellow peachy-looking fruit with a large stone covered in a tasty flesh but without the jakfruit's fragrance. One of our friends, Dr. Mo, despaired each season when faced with the prospect of having to remove accidentally swallowed indigestible santol seeds from children's rear ends – a very dedicated humane engineering feat.

A few lighter moments were provided at this time when we were invited to attend the weddings of various employees working on the new building. Often these were lavish family affairs with a party held at the bride's home after the church ceremony, where I was expected to make a speech. On one occasion however, the Guest of Honour was the newly appointed Archbishop of the Province of the Indian Ocean who sat and chatted with us throughout the meal – we didn't realise until later that this was our great anti-apartheid hero – Trevor Huddleston.

That same wedding celebration remains in our memory as the occasion when another of the guests, the Hospital matron, described the unexpected effect of having alerted one of her pregnant patients to the importance of increasing the iron in her diet. On a subsequent check-up she had still found indications of anaemia despite being assured that her advice was being followed. Closer enquiry revealed that the mother-to-be had been conscientiously been dosing herself with a 'tisane' made by boiling up a saucepan of rusty nails.

My career as an engineer came to an abrupt end that December. The eighteen month contract I had agreed to was terminated as a money-saving measure. John was kept on to chivvy the men along in a desperate attempt to get some of the hotel operational before the first unfortunate guests were due to arrive. It took a further three months to finish the hotel and there was a lot of bad press from the poor guests.

That I was not there to face the ire of both guests and management came as a great relief. There were other distractions on our minds – the prospect of a holiday in Cyprus in lieu of a bonus for my work over the past eighteen months, and the need to get some batiks finished for an exhibition that Gill and I were working towards at the Reef Hotel in January.

One thing was certain. I went home to Gill and Justin, who had his nose to the window in his bedroom, gazing at the hesitant steps of a bright green chameleon on an overhanging branch, and I never worked for anyone ever again.

The gallery at the Reef Hotel was on the first floor overlooking the restaurant and bar; it had an intimidating expanse of wall that we were expected to make best use of. Considering the frenzy of the past few months, we had managed to mount and frame thirty-five batiks, including two pieces three metres wide. Gill, who had been told by her school art teacher that she was hopeless at drawing and had no talent, had for this exhibition used her fine sense of colour to produce works of uncomplicated figure drawings brought to life by the most vibrant colours. My own choice of subject had

been the muscular labourers, fishermen, the drunks on the beach and my usual stock in trade – reef fish.

Hanging the odd painting among the work of others at Camion Hall or having a few on display at Vista do Mar was not in the least as scary as having all our own work on exhibition and having to face a crowd of viewers, however friendly, at an opening. In the minutes before the first guests were due to arrive on that nerve-wracked day in mid-January, Francesca, the exhibition organiser, tried to quell our fears; held our hands and assured us that we wouldn't be the only viewers that evening. She was right, of course, but even so, we were overwhelmed by the size of the crowd and the sudden appearance of red 'sold' labels next to some of the exhibits.

The Chief Minister had been persuaded to open the exhibition which suited his image as a rising star and man of the people; a happy, cheerful man who mixed freely with the public and always had time to chat and raise a laugh. He made a brief introduction highlighting the importance of the arts to the culture of the islands. He reminded me that the last time we had spoken, I was in my shorts and covered in cement dust at the Coral Strand, but neglected to mention that at that meeting he had been wandering about in his swim-suit. Formalities over, he was free to drift through the noisy crowd and put an arm around the shoulders of all the pretty girls.

The exhibition was a great success and we came away on closing day knowing that we could survive as artists, without the need to supplement our income by taking on meaningless boring jobs.

The sweet smell of success might have gone to our heads but for a small distraction that resulted in a few months of friendly teasing. It was all to do with one letter in the alphabet. The main publicity for the Reef exhibition appeared on the front page of the daily newspaper and included some biographical details about both of us. It stated that I was a 'wandering South African' – at least that's what it meant to say, but the proof reader, if they even employed one, hadn't noticed that the letter 'k' had slipped in, where the 'd' was supposed to be!

With the exhibition out of the way, we set about finding tenants to look after our house during our absence and began making preparations for our promised stay in Cyprus. It turned out to be a long roundabout journey because we had asked Grandma to accompany us. This involved a trip from Heathrow to Lytham St. Annes in Lancashire and a short wintery stay in her house. On Gill's birthday, the first day of spring, we took a day trip to the Lake District, to see the daffodils in 'Dora's Field' – Wordsworth's memorial to his daughter - before embarking at Heathrow for Cyprus.

Arriving at Nicosia airport we drove north to the apartment loaned to us on the outskirts of Ambelia, a tourist village on the mountainside overlooking the romantic port town of Kyrenia. We, who had read and loved every word Lawrence Durrell had ever written, now found ourselves in the heart of the Cyprus of his 'Bitter Lemons'. Not only were we here in Bellapaix, here was the monastery and there, the 'Tree of Idleness' with the old men sitting in its shade, some playing cards, others dreaming.

We were completely bowled over by the island. It was not at all like our tropical paradise but had its own magnificence; a wide open landscape unlike the dense tropical forests at home. Most of all, the people were warm, friendly and laughed easily as though life was a pleasure.

It was all too easy to get swept up in the dream of maybe finding an old village house and turning it into a home and gallery, living the good life in a country steeped in history and romance. We found a comfortable café and cake shop, installed Justin and Grandma, and did the rounds of the estate agents, eventually finding an easily affordable property in the village of Lapithos, at the same altitude as Bellapaix but some miles to the west of Kyrenia and facing Turkey. The property was probably a remnant of what had once been a large lemon orchard, now reduced in size to a village garden full of lemon trees. A narrow two storey building stood in one corner of the garden, more a barn than a house, but it had a clear view of the village below, the church and the winding coastline.

We went 'en famille' on the day we made our decision to buy it and were treated by the agent to a vast Cypriot feast down on the coast, a meal

that lasted so long, we began to wonder if we had agreed on too high a price. On the way back to Ambelia, still covered in honey and pastry crumbs from the baklava and not a little tiddly from all of the food and wine and the effects of the rich Commandaria dessert wine, the oldest named wine in the world, we felt a great contentment and could imagine living here. Justin was quite happy, peering out of the car window and pointing out all the "nanny goats" which were the subject of his current favourite bed-time story. Grandma, however, was not totally enamoured with our vision of her, with her knitting, sitting on a village doorstep with a group of black-clad old ladies, making lace. Despite being a prolific knitter who kept the family supplied with beautiful warm knitwear, she never assumed the role of little old lady knitting quietly in her rocking chair. Instead, she was at the centre of every conversation, and should it be outside her understanding, she demanded an explanation. Her strength of character was tempered by a keen sense of humour that kept us all on our toes. She definitely was not going to dress in black and sit on a Cypriot doorstep with the other old ladies of the village.

When we arrived home in Seychelles, stiff and sore from trying to sleep upright in the plane for thirteen hours, the house-sitters returned the keys and left us to recover in peace. All seemed well except for the missing cat – Catty, as Justin had chosen to name him with a three-year-old's creativity – who turned up next morning in the arms of a friend. Tiz said she had rescued poor little Catty because he had turned up at her home, high up in the hills, and was obviously in need of a little TLC. To judge by the knee-high pile of empty Fray Bentos steak and kidney pie tins in our garden, feeding cats and cooking creative meals had probably not been high on the list of our tenants' priorities. It is possible that they may have been put off cooking real food by our neighbour's Sunday ritual slaughter of screeching piglets.

We were all feeling a bit jet-lagged and while we would normally have read to Justin and put him to bed by six, that evening we sat him in an armchair on the veranda with Catty on his lap, to watch the spectacle of scores of fire-flies flashing their love signals through the house and garden in the inky black tropical night. The chattering of the fruit bats and the sound of the babbling stream soon lulled him off to sleep. It was good to be home.

Soon back to normal, we drove up to Mountain Rise to see Gisèle and Knud. We hadn't known what to bring them as a small gift from Europe, so had settled on a carton of cigarettes. They both smoked like chimneys and without their assistance the global tobacco industry might have collapsed.

Knud was no longer totally absorbed in his astrological calculations, having met some Italian investors with ideas for the future. He was in expansive mood and regaled us with stories of when they were part of the wild expat set in Kenya, their youthful exploits in Mombasa. When Knud was working on the new Kilindini harbour they had lived in what he said was a penthouse flat in the town and drove around in a pre-war Mercedes Benz which, as the smartest car in the town, had been requisitioned on one occasion for the use of the Kenyan President, Jomo Kenyatta. While Gisèle might have found their present circumstances a bit of a come-down, she always kept up appearances and like Knud, lived in the belief of better things to come "when our ship comes in".

A steady trickle of visitors found their way to our studio and someone from the tourism division was keen that we should be included in the itinerary of the fledgling tour companies. I was still spending the odd evening teaching at Camion Hall and was surprised one night on my return home to find Gill on top of the kitchen table, knife in hand, waving it frantically at the three-inch long flying cockroaches clattering around the lights and scuttling away on the floor, feelers waving this way and that. At least they didn't hiss like their larger relations in Madagascar. Swatting and squashing put an end to this invasion but Gill never got over her horror of cockroaches.

I had avoided giving private tuition at the studio. That is, until Gaia asked to be shown the rudiments of the batik waxing and dyeing process, a request I couldn't resist. One afternoon when she had decided that she would stick to drawing and painting rather than getting spattered with dye that couldn't be washed off, she and Joe told us that Alix, one of their colleagues at the Gigolette, had mentioned their plans for the schooling of his two young sons.

Apparently, his mother-in-law, a kindergarten teacher, had come to stay and was going to start a small nursery school to teach her grandsons and one or two other children of the same age. Gaia and Joe were keen to have their daughter, Natasha, included and did we think it would be good for Justin?

Alix and Anna and their two young boys, Simon and Daniel, lived at Pointe Conan where they ran a craft workshop with the name of NAK – the creole word for mother-of-pearl. Anna's mother, Elizabeth, planned to run the school on the covered porch at the back of the house. When we met her we knew immediately that we couldn't have wished for anyone better to start Justin's education. Elizabeth was gentle, calm and soft-spoken in a very precise way. The first day of school turned out to be quite traumatic with floods of tears all the way there and the pair of us worrying about what we had done to a little three-year-old. It turned out that the moment we had turned our backs, the crying ceased and Justin interested himself in what was going on.

Daily trips to school led to regular visits to Anna and Alix and sharing ideas on the craft business, so that in November, Anna and Gill had a joint exhibition at Camion Hall. Gill had concentrated on batik fabric clothing for children this time. The school group plus the niece of the dressmaker, Daphie, were the models at the opening. Anna and Alix showed their handmade jewellery and

crafts made from local materials. The exhibition was opened by the mother of the Chief Minister; a large imposing lady, mother of one politician, one pop singer, a daughter and three more sons who kept the family grocery business going.

A change in the weather

We had two family visits that year; my mother, my sister Rhona and her two girls, came to stay. We found rooms for Mom and Rhona nearby in Norman's Masonic Lodge. The girls were squeezed into Justin's room and he was displaced to our room, as happened later when Grandma came out again.

This was to be a very adventurous visit for Grandma. To start with, she developed severe toothache and had to be taken to Dr. Harter's dental surgery. We had got to know him quite well during Gill's pregnancy, when internal demands for calcium and our deprived diet at the time hadn't done her teeth any good. He was a very gentle, kind dentist and extremely concerned about Grandma when he discovered a tooth lying sideways in her gum.

She had recovered from the difficult extraction before Christmas Day when we had reserved a table at the Pirates Arms Hotel to partake of a family Christmas lunch. The Austrian chef was someone we knew from Vista do Mar but who had been poached (the culinary equivalent of head-hunted) by the new Austrian owners of the Pirates Arms and Poivre Island. We knew that we were going to enjoy a sumptuous meal.

Monsoon rain began to fall on Christmas Eve and continued all night and the next morning. The torrential downpour continued for hours, and the three-foot wide monsoon storm drains soon disappeared under a knee-deep lake in Victoria. We set out for our luxurious lunch smartly dressed, but by the time we reached the hotel we were soaking wet, with trousers rolled up and skirts tucked into knickers. The rain kept on and on throughout our very enjoyable lunch and the lake outside the window rose higher and higher. After we had eaten we splashed our way home through the floodwaters. The gentle murmuring stream in the garden had turned into a raging torrent with a roar not unlike the Victoria Falls. There was no log fire to warm us and no 'African Queen' on the television to relax in front of, because television had still not reached these remote islands.

Although we thought we were in for the Great Flood, there were occasional days when it all subsided and the sun came out and nature lapsed into its gentler self. On one of those sunny days we were invited to morning coffee at a friend's house. No sooner had we settled down with our coffee and biscuits than a marauding army of blue-black storm clouds came rushing over the horizon. Huge raindrops pattered down on the sodden ground, quite rapidly escalating into a thundering roar on the tin roof, so loud all conversation ceased.

When the storm subsided to a drizzle we decided to make a dash for home. Our route was barred at the Irish Bridge, where the road went under the water instead of over it. The muddy water was a thigh deep swirling river which was too deep to cross by car. It had started to rain again and we didn't know how long we would be stranded there. On the opposite bank stood the security of Gaia and Joe's house where we decided to take shelter. No point in rolling up trousers or tucking things in this time, we joined hands and waded into the maelstrom and struggled to the other bank and safety, absolutely soaked through but relieved to have avoided being swept away in the muddy torrent, never to be seen again.

Fortunately Gaia and Joe were at home and produced towels and dry clothes for us and decided to use a Nordic tradition to warm us up; wine-glasses filled to the brim with neat vodka. It was as well there were no breathalyzers in use when we rescued the car an hour later and drove home past the police station.

And it wasn't the end of Grandma's adventures. The combination of extreme humidity and heat provided the perfect conditions for tropical ulcers and boils. A nasty boil decided to develop on Grandma's rear end only days before she was due to be stuck, sitting down for thirteen hours on the flight home. It was enough to make her decide that she didn't much enjoy the tropics – despite the fascinated attention she received on returning to her own G.P in U.K.

The floods had well and truly subsided by late January when I held my first one-man show at the Pirates Arms, concentrating on the fishermen of Beau Vallon with several life-sized batiks. It was, in a way, a parting shot at arts and crafts in Seychelles for us. For some months we had become obsessed with the idea of the house conversion in Cyprus and when the partner that Gaia and Joe had taken on at the Gigolette expressed an interest in buying our little house, who were we to say 'no'. The person most put out by our decision to leave the islands was Gisèle who thought of us as her own family.

The most bitter lemon

We took a round-about route to get to Cyprus. We spent some days in Sri Lanka touring the island, visiting Sygiria and Kandy and enjoying the Galle Face Hotel in Colombo. We flew from there to Karachi where we changed airlines for the onward leg to Teheran. This was an Aeroflot flight with frightening alarm signals at take off, empty seats that flopped down as we scooted along the runway and in-flight orange juice and an apple for lunch.

Iran was beyond our expectations. Teheran was, we thought, like a middle eastern version of Paris, with its fashionably dressed women, rather frightening traffic and the food, though simple, really delicious. We made a long bus trip down to Isfahan through the desert and stayed in the Arab splendour of the Shah Abbas hotel and wandered through the covered market, searching for a Persian rug. On our return to Teheran we took a flight to war-torn Beirut and onwards to Nicosia.

We rented a modest newly built house a few miles to the west of Kyrenia. It was square and boxlike with the obligatory arrangement of reinforcing bars poking out of the flat roof; this being an indication that the house was still under construction and was therefore not liable for taxation.

The plans I had drawn up for the house in Lapithos were passed on to an architect recommended by the estate agent, who would submit them for planning permission; a bureaucratic process that was no doubt going to rush along at a snail's pace. We realised that we had time on our hands, time to spend finding an outlet for our batiks and laying a foundation that would publicise our proposed new studio at Lapithos.

On our previous visit we had met an artist couple in Bellapaix who had suggested that we talk to the owner of a gallery in Kyrenia about exhibiting some of our batiks. Much to our relief he plied us with tiny cups of

Turkish coffee and said he welcomed the idea of having something different in the gallery. His suggestion was that as his clients were for the most part tourists, he would like to start with two or three pieces with a local theme.

Inspiration was everywhere; in the village doorways, in the squares under the trees of idleness and around Kyrenia harbour where there were characters just as inspiring as the fishermen on Beau Vallon beach. The very dry climate was conducive to working outdoors; I no longer had to rush out in tropical downpours to rescue the dyeing. It was also a reminder that in the tropics, the constant humidity invaded even closed spaces like cupboards and wardrobes where the smell of must and mildew was endemic and mould grew on any worn garment, but especially on shoes. The dryness and resultant limited access to water in Cyprus also made gardening a problem once we had started collecting cuttings for the garden at Lapithos which we grew in cut-off milk cartons and watered sparingly with our precious water. Lemon trees seemed to thrive in spite of the dry, producing a large crop on our land which Gill converted into gallons of homemade lemonade; a different flavour from the lime-ade we were used to in Seychelles.

With our money safely transferred to the bank in Kyrenia and everything set in motion for the renovation and extension of the Lapithos house, we took ourselves off to London. We went to a car showroom in Knightsbridge and spent the small fortune of £900 on a brand new Renault 4.

We drove up to see Grandma, stopping off in Ashton-under-Lyne to visit Gill's college friend, Jo, and her Greek-Cypriot husband, Andreas. It was he who told us about what seemed to be minor political rumblings that had surfaced once more in Cyprus. The political infighting probably wasn't going to touch us, or so we thought.

After the student uprising at the end of November in Greece, there had been a coup in Athens in which the original Greek junta had been replaced by the Chief of Military Police, Brigadier Ioannides. He suspected Makarios of being a communist sympathizer. This led Ioannides to support a plot to undermine Makarios.

On July 2nd Makarios, sensing trouble, had ordered that Greece remove some 600 Greek officers of the Cypriot National Guard from Cyprus. The Greek Government's reply was to order the go-ahead of the coup. On 15th July, sections of the Cypriot National Guard, led by its Greek officers, overthrew the government.

We set off on our Cyprus odyssey blissfully unaware of the gravity of the situation. Our slow leisurely journey took us through France to Andorra in the Pyrenees, along the Mediterranean coast to Italy by way of the interesting sites for Justin; the Pont d'Avignon in France and the Colosseum in Rome. We caught the ferry to Patras from Brindisi and drove across the Peleponnese to see Agamemnon's tomb and Epidaurus, and on to Athens and Piraeus – our departure point for Cyprus.

Makarios narrowly escaped death in the attack. He fled the presidential palace by catching a taxi after escorting a party of school children out of the building and went to Paphos where the British managed to pick him up by helicopter and flew him from Akrotiri to Malta and from there to London where he arrived on 17th July. Makarios was arriving in London on the very day we boarded the ferry to Limassol.

It was then that we remembered what Andreas had said. We also wished we had re-read 'Bitter Lemons' with Lawrence Durrell's concerns about Enosis and EOKA's uprising during his stay on the island. We couldn't understand the headlines on the Greek newspapers but gleaned from what we could translate that there was a war in Cyprus – a coup d'état in fact, not a war. At least, not yet a war. All over the ship's deck sat little huddled groups of people, poring over transistor radios relaying the BBC World Service news. The ferry company was apparently expecting it all to be sorted by the next morning when we were due to disembark.

We spent a hideously uncomfortable night in an inside cabin with no way of escaping the oppressive heat. As the sun rose into a pale cloudless sky, the ferry dropped anchor in the approach to the harbour and waited for instructions from a very nervous harbour master. We considered staying on board as the ferry was bound next for Haifa in Israel, but eventually we were allowed to join the disembarking Cypriot passengers, collect our car and head for the nearest hotel.

This was Thursday morning 18th July, and we made the best of the situation, enjoyed the swimming pool and the perfect weather, but like good expats, mostly sat glued to the BBC as the news slowly unfolded and swapped concerns with other worried hotel guests. The major threat seemed not to be the internal upheaval but the likelihood of a Turkish invasion. The coup leaders must have felt that they had control of the situation because the next morning people were allowed to go about their daily business but with a night time curfew in force.

After breakfast we piled into our little Renault 4 and headed north, over the mountains to Kyrenia. The presence of armed men and tanks on the road didn't help to calm our jangling nerves one little bit. About midday we reached Kyrenia and were relieved to see the bank was still open. The manager laughed when we asked if he wasn't worried about the Turks invading. He threw his arms in the air and said, in a very matter of fact way,

"Turks? Turks? Oh, please. They are always saying these stupid things but they never come. Don't worry, you are safe here."

Safe or not, it took us a while to persuade him to let us have a bank cheque for all the money we had deposited. We promised to return in a week with his cheque if he proved to be right. There wasn't much to collect from the rented house, but we made the detour in any case and then set off at top speed in order to get back to the hotel before the night-time curfew. Once in the safety of our hotel room we pounced on the radio and tuned into the Beeb; our most reliable Auntie.

Meantime Nikos Sampson had been declared provisional president of the new government. A Greek ultra-nationalist who was known to be fanatically anti-Turkish. His regime took over radio stations and declared that Makarios had been killed, although, safe in London, Makarios was soon able to counteract these reports.

The Turkish-Cypriots were unaffected by the coup against him; one of the reasons was that Ioannides did not want to provoke a Turkish reaction. Turkey, however, did not receive the guarantees it sought and took matters into their own hands.

During the night, news came through that the Turks had landed on the north of the island and by dawn a full-scale battle was underway. Sitting in the lounge waiting for instructions we were horrified when a truck rushed up to the hotel entrance and the hotel staff were despatched to fetch bedsheets which they told us were needed for use as bandages.

Forty-eight hours after disembarking from the ferry, we were sitting in our car in a slow-moving convoy en route to the British base at Akrotiri. There were men with guns everywhere, looking menacing then a sudden crackle of gunfire nearby almost frightened us out of our wits.

We had given a lift to another hotel guest who was sitting in the back of the car with Justin. He gently put his hand on Justin's head and quietly said to him:

"If I suddenly put my hand on your head like this, you must duck down onto the floor". That said, he offered Gill a cigarette but they were both shaking so much it was impossible to share his lighter!

The temperature outside was around forty degrees Celsius and probably twice that in the car. We could not tell what was sweat or what was fear. Along the roadside we passed isolated small cars, including several Renault 4s, boiling away and unable to go any further, their owners having been picked up by other motorists.

There was a general confused milling crowd at Akrotiri but somehow the service personnel managed to establish some sort of order, produced a list of refugees and divided us into groups for the evacuation flights back to England. In the midst of this confusion I had wandered off to find something for Justin to drink when our number came up. Gill, still in her bikini and sarong after our sudden departure from the hotel, was thrown into more panic as she tried to find me before the transport left without us. We made it by a cat's whisker, boarded the military VC10 (with its seats all facing backwards) and waved good-bye to our car sitting sadly in the vast car park with all the other abandoned vehicles.

The ground staff at RAF Brize Norton, with ladies from the WVS, were waiting for us. They were kind and understanding; offered us food and even money if we needed it. They had organised hire cars for anyone who needed transport. A little rested after the flight, we set off in our hired car for Steve and Stephanie's home in Manchester, arriving there in the early hours of the morning.

"Thank God for that!", said Steve, opening the door in his pyjamas. "We've spent the last week trying to convince Grandma that there was absolutely no chance you were anywhere near Cyprus!"

We were back in Seychelles three days later. Cyprus, no longer a romantic dream, had been more like a very bitter lemon.

Chapter 5

<u>Some small miracles</u>

The sun was gently bleaching the early morning reds and oranges from the clouds over the Indian Ocean as the plane began its descent towards Seychelles. The colonial service couple in the seats in front of us were having a heated argument about something important.

"Don't go on about it", he grumbled.

"I asked you, and you ignored me. All I wanted was to buy a cauliflower to bring back to this God-forsaken place – this land where all you get in the shops is "Napa" – none, none, none and nothing."

"Oh! Stop your bloody nagging, you can always pack it in and go home; I have a contract to fulfil."

Gill poked me in the ribs and stage whispered,

"Welcome back to the things that really matter and where the drama in Cyprus is of no importance."

Late July was in the middle of the holiday season and we were lucky to find a room at Vista do Mar where we stayed until we could find a house to rent. Most of the people we knew were unaware that we had even been away, but Gisèle and Knud were pleased to see us safe and sound and could sympathise, having experienced the war in Europe and later the Mau-Mau rebellion in Kenya.

We found a house near the beach at Beau Vallon. It was fairly basic but included a large open-sided garage under the same roof, with a door opening directly into the kitchen. It was the obvious place for a workshop and studio, which we had up and running within days of moving in. Justin was back at Elizabeth's school with his chums, none the worse for all the travelling and the excitement in Cyprus.

Gisèle invited us to lunch at their new abode. They had moved from Mountain Rise to a house much further up the Sans Soucis road. It was a modern house with uninterrupted views of the chain of small islands that protected the Victoria anchorage and on clear days, the more distant islands of Praslin, La Digue, Recife and Fregate.

While Gisèle busied herself preparing a sumptuous meal in her new modern kitchen, Knud plied us with drinks and enthused about his new Italian contacts. They had bought a large piece of land at Danzilles and wanted him to design a hotel for them. The way Knud described their promises to him of long term association, their property buying spree and weird family set-up, made it sound as though he had found himself a Sicilian godfather.

In this run-up to independence for Seychelles – the inevitability of which had been accepted by all political parties the previous year – overseas 'investors' had come to these pristine shores with their money and big ideas. There was already a vast building that looked like an ocean liner stranded on the rocks at Port Glaud on the west coast, the Mahé Beach Hotel.

It was not only Knud who was carried away by these exciting developments. Peter and Linda were heavily involved with a consortium of investors who had bought a huge tract of land at Baie Lazare at an inflated price, upon which they wished to build the first Sheraton hotel on the islands. There was talk of a large hotel on the tranquil Cote d'Or beach on Praslin and even the tiny island of Cousine had been sold to a developer. It all felt as if by magic the genie had been let out of the bottle labelled 'Property Development'.

Magic and miracles were what we too survived on. We, who made and sold things that no-one really needed, were always amazed to meet enthusiastic buyers of what we created.

Soon after our return, I had started work on what I thought of as a pseudo-mythical series of batiks. I was using the idea first proposed by General Gordon of Khartoum fame. He suggested that the palms which produced the strange double-lobed Coco de Mer nuts were the Trees of Knowledge and that Praslin, where the palms grew, was a fragment of the Garden of Eden. These were fertile grounds then for mythical symbols – there were the fairly innocuous endemic wolf snakes, the female Coco de Mer palm producing a fruit that resembled female buttocks and the male palm with its huge phallic protuberance covered in small flowers. Our own studio logo was a symbol of the phoenix, to do with the fire and molten wax we used. It was a spread-eagled black parrot rising from the flames, clutching the symbol of creation in each claw – a coco de mer.

Lost in a dream one afternoon, my nose close to the fabric as I guided my tjanting wax-drawing instrument around an intricate pattern in the design, I was suddenly aware of someone standing behind me, looking over my shoulder. A well-dressed man, about my own age, smiled at me and beckoned his wife to come closer.

"That's amazing", he said, then "Leila, come and have a look."

"Explain what it is and what you are doing", he added, after she had joined him.

I explained the batik technique and they listened attentively. A few days later they came back and introduced themselves. He was Hans, a German, and she, Leila, was Italian.

"I have a close friend in Italy who has an art gallery. If I can persuade him, would you consider having a show in Milan?" Hans asked.

"I can't believe what you've just asked me," was my response, once my feet had touched the ground again.

"Yes, please, please. I can't believe this is really happening."

Three weeks later a letter came from Hans, asking if I could be ready by the first week in May.

Preparations for the exhibition had to be worked around a commitment we had made to participate in a big craft fair to be held in the recently built stadium in February, to coincide with a visit to Seychelles of two cruise liners, the *Oronsay* and the *QE2*. It seemed a good idea to team up with Anna and Alix and have a single stall. Their woven baskets and mats made of natural local materials combined with their shell jewellery would work well with our hand-dyed cotton fabrics. The craft fair ran for two days and as always was accompanied by ear-splitting 'background' music which continued at its mind-numbing volume even when Jimmy, the Chief Minister, spent half an hour in the role of disc jockey. Our first prize for the best stall gave us food for thought. What if…? What if we joined forces and opened our own shop in Victoria?

A shop on the corner

It was spring when we arrived in the northern hemisphere; the daffodils were in full bloom and the sun tried vainly to convince us that the cold weather was over.

When we arrived at the Il Cannochiale Art Gallery on the Via Brera in Milan, around the corner from La Scala Opera House, we realised for the first time that this wasn't a little gallery tucked away in a shopping centre.

It was a major gallery in the heart of Milan's art world. The visitors were students, artists, opera singers, teachers and professors from the nearby Accademia who were interested, kind and complimentary; all of which made it a humbling experience to be accepted in such artistic company. Sales at the show paid for the not inconsiderable expense of staging an exhibition.

Shortly before our departure for the Milan exhibition, Elizabeth had told us that she was returning to the UK and we had arranged to rent her house next door to Anna and Alix at Pointe Conan on our return. This move also prompted us to look seriously at the possibility of a joint venture as shop owners. Alix found a vacant shop on the corner of what were then Royal and Quincy Streets, on the edge of the main shopping area in town. We heard of an elderly lady who had been working in a dress shop called 'Madame and Eve', who was more than willing to act as 'Manager' of 'Things', as we had decided to call our shop.

When we told Knud and Gisèle about our elderly shopgirl, there was, at first, a stony silence.

"Lady Mabs? You be careful, she can be quite vitriolic" this from Gisèle.

Knud cast his eyes heavenward and gave an exaggerated shiver.

"Mabs isn't Lady anything in any case. She was the old man's housekeeper and came here from India pretending they had been married."

We never did find out what Lady Mabs had said to all and sundry about Gisèle and Knud, but we were on our guard. She was always pleasant with us but we were aware that she enjoyed nothing more than a good gossip. She, the Queen of our shop, held court there regularly with most of the very elderly ex-India and Kenya colonials, some of them thin as rakes as though they hadn't eaten properly in ages. The Major often called, accompanied by his lady, trailing an equally skinny miniature dachshund on a lead or tucked under her arm.

Lady Mabs often kept us entertained with her memories of the good old days in India, some of them providing an insight into how the expats lived while others, like the toast story, needed a large pinch of salt. She told us how one morning the breakfast table had been set; all the ingredients for a hearty breakfast were assembled on the table, except for the toast. She'd stormed off to the kitchen to chivvy the staff along, only to discover the toast wallah sitting down with legs outstretched and his feet almost in the open fire. Clasped between his toes were slices of gently toasting bread. Understandably, it didn't make it as far as the table on that particular morning.

One of the advantages of having a shop in town was that we reached a wider audience and that Lady Mabs could direct visitors to our studio. The interior designer for the Mahé Beach Hotel was one such redirected visitor; he was looking for local art to decorate the walls of the rather large main restaurant. He wished to commission a series of large panels, a commission we were pleased to accept once we finally agreed on seabirds as the main subject.

Little did we realise what an enormous task we had taken on. It would involve applying wax to eight lengths of fabric, each the size of a double bed sheet. Each piece would then have to be dyed several times and when all the wax and dyes had been applied, we would have to immerse each piece in boiling water to remove the wax.

The dye bath came from Alix's father who was in charge of the prison at Union Vale. It was a large rubber trough from the milking parlour at the prison farm. The vessel for boiling out was a very large aluminium pan known locally as a 'soufrier' and we must have used about fifty packets of wax candles, several kilos of beeswax and our entire stock of dyes.

It was purely by chance that as I was about to embark on this commission, Knud asked me to accompany him on a trip to Cousine Island where he had been asked to advise on some structural elements of the houses being built there. The owner of the island had employed Jean-Pierre, one of the two Swiss lads I had met back in 1968, to design several houses on this, his private island. The houses were built into the landscape using rock walls to blend in with the natural granite-dominated hillside and they were to have flat concrete roofs that would allow the encroachment of vegetation to camouflage the houses.

We were met on the beach by Jean-Pierre and his girl Friday, Janet, who gave us coffee in their rustic quarters. Knud only made it as far as the first of the houses a couple of metres uphill, decided what needed to be done and then retreated to the shelter on the beach and a welcome cold beer with Janet. Jean-Pierre went off to supervise the builders while I took my camera and sketch pad on a wander around the island, mesmerised by the masses of noddy terns fluttering in and out of the casuarinas trees, trailing bits of nesting material. Contrasting with the brown plumage of the noddies were the pure white fairy terns and the tropic birds with what looked like mascara trailing off behind their eyes. Overhead frigate bird hung motionless on sickle-shaped wings, on the look-out for flying fish. These birds were the perfect subject for those huge panels for the Mahé Beach. The peacock I used on the panel behind the reception desk was, however, pure fantasy.

On good work days we sometimes treated ourselves and the children to a meal at the newly opened Italian-owned Continental Restaurant. Justin and the boys had what was for them a new culinary experience – pizza, while we indulged in other Italian specialities. Looking back on it now I still marvel at our choice of a reasonably priced wine – Chateauneuf du Pape, if you please!

One evening Alix invited us over to their house for a meal. There were what appeared to be about two dozen roasted quails on the table.

"Where on earth did you find quails, Alix", we asked.

"Not quails", he said with a big smile, "Pigeons."

"Your pigeons?"

"Yes, and some from the Chinese man along the road. You've seen how I let them out every evening, how they fly about for a while, then come home? Well, the last few days they have brought some Chinese visitors back with them. I've spent all day trying to give them back to him and also to give my pigeons away but no one wants them. So, here they are, they're good to eat, as any Seychellois will tell you."

While we were dealing with these delicious little piles of bony 'faux quails', Alix told us that he had spent a good part of the morning looking for William, the man who tidied the garden. When he did eventually locate him, William was pushing a wheelbarrow piled high with rotting potatoes that he had rescued from a rather overdue shipment that Temooljee's shop had dumped nearby. This was an island problem, where imported fruit and veg often arrived with long growing shoots that had developed during over-long sea voyages.

William apparently had a grin from ear to ear and answered Alix with a toothy leer, "La Puré!" These two words brought joy to the after-work, sometimes before-work and even sometimes, during work drinking men. It was a lethal brew made from rotting fruit or vegetables or anything that would accelerate fermentation. It was even more potent than Bacca, a local type of rum.

Following the completion of the Mahé Beach commission, I had been asked to make several life sized batiks for a new Italian restaurant called 'La Tartaruga Felice'. Guido and Ada sometimes invited us to eat at the restaurant but it was more often a case of eating the proceeds from the batiks we made for them. On several occasions we saw Jimmy, our Chief Minister, having a meal there. He was always friendly no matter who he was with. And so, it came as a surprise one day when an official car arrived at the studio and I was instructed that the Chief Minister demanded my presence. The young driver set off in a rush, telling me in no uncertain terms, almost as though I was one of the La Puré drinkers, how I should behave.

When I was ushered into Jimmy's presence he was his usual affable friendly self, not in the least as self-opinionated as his driver. All he wanted to know was, "as an artist", did I object to the idea of Guido painting the words 'La Tartaruga Felice' on the wall at the entrance to the restaurant. For no apparent reason, this sign had been objected to by the Führer of the Planning Department – a colonial servant with a reputation for his unreasonable attitude. I didn't object; Guido and Ada were cultured people and the sign would be modest. There was no lecture on the way back to the studio, but nevertheless it felt as though we needed a holiday.

Icarus and other flights of fancy

The opportunity to take that much needed holiday was decided for us by way of a letter informing us that our little Renault 4, long abandoned at Akrotiri Air Force base on Cyprus, was due for shipment to Venice and would we make arrangements to collect it. Who wouldn't want to go to Venice? Such a beautiful city and such superb food. Such a strange sight at the port too – our little car lifted in a sling and deposited on the quayside one cold, damp February evening. It was still full of our belongings, except for the rug from Isfahan.

We had planned to spend a month on Sardinia, but set off from Venice in a southerly direction towards the hills behind Rome. We were on our way to look at Count Spanni's castle which he wanted to sell. He was an acquaintance of Gaia and Joe, living on Praslin and in need of money. It turned out to be more like a vast coaching inn than a castle, with rows of stables at ground level and a multitude of rooms upstairs, some with elegant murals and frescoes. He was asking a mere five thousand pounds for it, but even we, with our heads in the clouds, knew that to renovate it would need one hundred times that sum.

We came into Rome on the old Appian Way and made our way to Civitavecchia where we boarded the ferry to Sardinia. We had rented a house on the Costa Smeralda and had invited Grandma and Steve, Stephanie and baby Kathy to stay with us for part of the time. My main interest was to prepare some sketches for work to be exhibited at a one-man show in Genoa the following year. For this exhibition I wanted to create something less like souvenirs of Seychelles; something more European. My interest in symbolism and mythology at the time had drawn me inevitably to the story of wax-winged Icarus and his flight too close to the sun.

However tenuous, I dreamt that I had risen Icarus-like on wax wings from making souvenirs to the rarefied atmosphere of the art world, although in danger of crashing back into the world of souvenir makers. The gnarled, twisted juniper trees with their slender twigs reaching towards the heavens appeared to be Icarus, molten-winged, falling to the earth. His fallen figure was everywhere in the rocky coastline and in the driftwood logs half-covered in sand, soothed and washed gently by the surging tides.

At the end of our Sardinian holiday we made our way back to Lytham St. Annes by way of a few days in Corsica and then the long drive across France. It was while we were staying with Grandma, preparing to return to Seychelles, that we found somewhere to spend the money we had put aside for Count Spanni's castle. We found an old stone barn ready for conversion in the tiny Yorkshire Dales village of Malham. We hadn't really thought about the need for a home away from Seychelles, but we were probably hedging our bets in case independence turned out to be another bitter lemon.

There was an air of optimism and excitement when we returned to Seychelles. Independence was soon to be a reality, prosperity would follow and we would all benefit. Even the political adversaries had put aside their differences, shaken hands and agreed to form a coalition.

Although we were very happy living next door to Anna and Alix, we could not resist the temptation when a large old house at the entrance to the new Beau Vallon Bay hotel became vacant. It had been the living quarters for the expat engineers building the hotel. There were  five bedrooms, a huge sitting room complete with a large built-in bar - an ideal room for the gallery - and only one bathroom with four toilets, four wash-basins and one bath; ideally suited for two adults and one child. There was also a ten foot wide veranda running the full width of the building, suitable for a working studio. The mucky jobs like dyeing and boiling out the wax could be confined to the garden at the back of the house.

One of our acquaintances at the time we moved into our new premises was Lari, an American who lived up on the hillside at Le Niol with her husband Chuck and their four sons. Chuck was often away, representing Random House books, or so he said. Rumour had it that with all his comings and goings he was actually working for the CIA.

Lari was the spark that got us looking for clay suitable for pottery making; one of the ideas I had delved into before we came to live on the islands. We didn't really know how to assess the quality of the abundant clay that we found, but tried as best we could to produce something useful. We were helped by an elderly art teacher, Mrs. Thomas, a Russian lady who always wore a black polo-necked sweater and black trousers, no matter the Seychelles temperature. Mrs. Thomas had an electric kiln and used imported clay but was interested in our search for a local source of clay.

We were put to shame though, when a South African couple set up a pottery studio at Glacis. Russell was an excellent potter and knew exactly what good clay looked like in its raw form. He and wife Jill found bands of really good clay on Praslin and at Glacis with which they produced some fine pieces. We had some examples of Russell's pottery on display in our gallery alongside some beautifully crafted inlaid wooden boxes that were made by Chris, one half of a young English couple with a small daughter.

Pauline, his wife, was a VSO volunteer, a social worker and teacher who was involved in broadcasting educational radio programmes. Her help in pairing up with Gisèle to run the gallery and feed the cats when we were away was invaluable.

'While we were messing about, the day of Independence was looming large. In late May we were visited by staff from the protocol department, wishing to place an order for two batik pictures to be presented to the Duke and Duchess of Gloucester, who were to represent the Queen at the Independence celebrations. As an added bonus, we were also to be included as a stop on their tour of the island.

When that day dawned we were all clean and tidy, Justin was spick and span, his hair neatly brushed. Gisèle would have been proud of us. Gill and I were in our best ironed casuals and I even had shoes and socks on to hide my multi-coloured dyed feet. I had tried wearing wellies to do the dyeing, but they only filled up with dye to ankle depth.

The visit went without a hitch, they were gracious and charming and might have stayed longer had the protocol people not been jumping up and down, anxious to keep to the schedule.

On the evening of 28th June, the Seychelles populace was making its way to the stadium to witness the ceremonial Flag-Raising Ceremony which would take place on the stroke of midnight. Rows and rows of tropical uniformed troops from Britain as well as various well-wishing countries were in attendance, the Seychelles police band was there, together with the futurePresident and Prime Minister as well as the retiring colonial Governor.

We were celebrating with Gisèle and Knud, high up on the mountainside with a view of all the ships in the harbour. Knud had his fingers crossed in the hope that the police band would repeat an earlier faux pas when they launched into the opening bars of

'Show me the Way to go Home' instead of the National Anthem. Instead, as midnight approached, the stand-up-straight, chest-out strains of 'God Save the Queen' heralded the slow coming down to earth of the Union Jack and the raising of our new flag, to the far jollier tune of 'En Avant', our new republic's anthem.

From the anchorage and echoing off the mountainside came the eerie howls of the flotilla of naval vessels sounding their horns in celebration, like a pack of wolves baying at the moon. A most moving event, to be present at the birth of a new nation. We toasted the future and all felt very emotional.

The wolves were an omen we were too excited to heed on this dawn of our flight of fancy into what Jimmy, our former Chief Minister, promised would be a future where he would take to the world stage to sell Seychelles to the tourism industry and attract the rich and famous to our shores.

The next morning, the 29th of June 1976, the sun rose as was its habit, revealing scattered light clouds hastening across the blue sky ahead of the strong south-east trade-winds. These were good omens for the day that was designated Seychelles Independence Day.

There was a steady stream of pedestrians and all the buses and camions the island could muster, heading to the stadium where the official handing over ceremony was to take place.

A small red, white and blue covered marquee had been erected for the Duke and Duchess and the important dignitaries. All the ladies were in their best summer dresses, hats and white gloves, the men in suits and ties and the governor, white uniformed and crowned with his splendid many plumed helmet.

Lesser dignitaries were seated in rows in the shade on the grandstand, while the rest of us, mere mortals, filled the terraces. Seated in front of the grandstand facing the marquee were again, row upon row of glaring white naval uniforms representing many different countries.

There followed an afternoon filled with an entire parliament of speeches, poetry from our new President and flags fluttering around the stadium. The President and Prime Minister swore the Oath of Allegiance to the new nation; the President with his right hand, the Prime Minister with his left. The band played, the people cheered and waved their new flags.

Birds of a feathery sort

The excitement of Independence Day had hardly subsided when a tall elegant man with a shock of blonde hair brought his wife to the gallery.

They had recently been on La Digue island and we fell into a discussion about the birdlife of the island. When they left, they had paid by cheque for several purchases, including a batik of the black paradise flycatcher, a rare bird found only on La Digue.

"Who was that?"

"Not sure. There's something very familiar about him but I can't put my finger on it."

"Isn't he that chap who…?"

"Who what? Maybe he's something theatrical, certainly has the voice for it."

"Oh, wait a minute. Here's his cheque. Here it is – he's Michael Heseltine. What does he do?"

"Pass me those magazines."

Those magazines included 'The Economist' which we subscribed to for a while as it gave us a lot more detailed news than we got from the BBC World Service.

"Aha!" said Gill, waving the magazine for me to see.

"He's Shadow Environment Minister. Maybe his interest in wildlife had something to do with that."

The U.K. had a Labour government at the time but we weren't likely to forget Michael Heseltine for one reason or another in the future.

Later in the year we received a surprise invitation to attend the opening ceremony of the Pan African Ornithological Congress that was to be held in Seychelles at the newly-opened Mahé Beach Hotel. The reason for the invitation was a bit of a mystery because, although I had a life-long passion for birds, I was a little intimidated by the scientific community's ownership of all the bird projects. Maybe, just maybe, the bird panels in the main restaurant of the hotel had something to do with the invitation?

There was a large notice at the entrance, put there to calm many of the excited delegates. It said:

"All the buzzards you have reported today are in fact fruit bats!"

Our President had been invited to open the Congress, an invitation he had accepted as it gave him an international platform to promote a different aspect of the natural beauty of Seychelles. He had begun to attract criticism in some quarters for his need to be in the public eye and for the young ladies he attracted. This evening though, he was in a more sombre mood. The sea of strange people who had not the slightest interest in tourism or politics may have put him off his stride and caused him to fluff his first line.

He was here, he said, "to open the orinth – orthin - Orthinological Congress". It was a short introduction and, unusually, he did not include any poetry. As soon as dinner was over the birders got down to the business of migration, breeding and discoveries that would occupy them for the next two weeks.

A few weeks later we had a visit from one of the participants we had met at the Congress. Jeff was a graduate from Aberdeen University, studying the Seychelles kestrels for his PhD. At the time of his visit he had gone off at a tangent, looking at the only other bird of prey in the islands; the diminutive Seychelles scops owl. He had teamed up with a young lady called Sharon who was a photographer and had taken the first ever photographs of the owl. During their visit we had to deal with other visitors to the gallery and Jeff spent the time showing Justin the photographs and talking to him about owls.

Some weeks later we went to visit them at the house they rented near L'Exile, high up on the ridge of the mountain. We heard the husky croaking call of the owls, but were not lucky enough to see them.

Towards the end of November we took a brief trip to South Africa, leaving Gisèle and Pauline in charge of the gallery. It was the first time we had been to South Africa in six years and was a chance to show Justin some of the sights and introduce him to those family members he had not met before. There were the wild animals and birds to see, the man-made hole at Kimberley and the Thomas the Tank Engine steam trains whose lines often ran parallel to the road and provided our young passenger with an opportunity to wave to the engine drivers.

When we arrived back at the airport in Seychelles, the man at the immigration desk took my very valued and hard-won British passport, and put a great big stamp across the window on the cover. It said, in no uncertain terms, CANCELLED. My jaw dropped, but not as far as my poor beating heart. I had fulfilled all the requirements about length of stay in the UK and Colonies, I was married to a very English rose and I had even stood in the Governor's office and sworn allegiance to the Queen. And now what? It seems that when Idi Amin Dada had expelled all the Asian population from Uganda and they became Britain's responsibility, the U.K. government had decided not be caught with its pants down a second time. In future, anyone born or naturalised in a colony would automatically become a citizen of that independent country and lost their entitlement to a British passport.

In the new year, Justin started to attend the International School with Simon. This was a privately-run school set up initially to educate the children of colonial service people in preparation for their eventual return to the British school system. It also attracted other expat children and those locals whose children were not in the catholic schools.

We, meanwhile, were busy preparing for the forthcoming exhibition in Genoa. It wasn't all plain sailing because we were in the middle of the North-west monsoon rains which involved a lot of running in and out, rescuing the dyeing.

It was, however, the perfect weather for indoor visits by centipedes, moths, flying ants, cockroaches and thousands of tiny zinging mosquitoes. We burned Moon Tiger coils in all the rooms but as soon as they were burned out the zinging resumed. Some of these nasty little creatures had become carriers of Dengue fever and one of them found an unprotected arm or leg on Gill and put her in bed for the best part of two weeks. It is a horribly debilitating fever, sometimes called break-back fever because of severe pain in the back and limbs, followed by several weeks of extreme weakness. The only positive aspect, if there can be a positive side effect from Dengue, was that Gill, who had smoked countless cigarettes each day, never smoked again. We would not however recommend this as a pleasant way to stop smoking.

In April we set off on another roundabout journey, this time to Genoa, going first to the U.K. to collect the car and Grandma.

The gallery where I was to exhibit my Icarus pictures was not quite as prestigious as the gallery in Milan, but was well-patronised. It was called Il Punto and was on the first floor of a building on the Piazza Colombo. As in Milan, we were quite overcome by the Italian warmth and enthusiasm at the exhibition preview.

We were not expected to spend every day in the gallery and so decided to take a short break in Tunisia. On our arrival at the port in Tunis, much to the consternation of Gill and Grandma, I was marched off to the immigration police office by two scowling officers who were not at all impressed with my brand new Seychelles passport, No. 00072.

"What is this Sey-chelles?" they demanded.

"Well, it's some islands."

"Islands? What's islands??" getting more and more aggressive.

"Islands in the Indian Ocean."

"India?"

"No, not India. See, here is Africa, here is Madagascar, here Mauritius."

"You sit here, wait", pointing at a hard wooden bench.

About an hour later, a smiling officer returned.

"Ah, yes. Sey-chelles, member of Organisation of African Unity. Very good. You go now!"

We shot off at high speed bound for Hammamet down the coast. It was an interesting break, especially for Justin when we visited the Roman Coliseum to the south and the ruins of Carthage near Tunis. At one point we also thought we might lose Grandma when an elderly gentleman began to take an interest in her. She was flattered but not at all inclined, she informed us, to take up with some-one just because he needed to have his washing done and his socks darned.

By early June we were back in Lytham and making the odd trip up to Malham to see how work was progressing on the conversion of our old 1709 barn. Anna and Alix were also in England on holiday and had been to visit us there in that lovely part of the Yorkshire dales.

A few days later on 5th June 1977 we heard on the BBC that there had been

a coup d'état in Seychelles while the President was away in London to attend the Commonwealth conference.

President Jimmy was replaced by his long-standing political rival, France Albert Rene, who had been Prime Minister in the coalition government which had lasted less than a year before this violation of the country's Constitution.

Slowly we learned the details. Armed supporters of the SPUP, Seychelles People's United Party, had attacked and captured two police stations in Victoria and seized the armoury. Two members of the police force were killed. The broadcasting station was soon in rebel hands. As there was no army, once the police had capitulated to the new regime, the coup was complete. A curfew was imposed and the Chief Justice, an Irish citizen, was expelled. Five British policemen on secondment to the Seychelles were deported, including the 'stayed on' head of security whose car we had once scraped and who had threatened to deport us, and who now found himself deported back to the U.K.

Chapter 6

<u>Troubled times in paradise</u>

These were very confusing times for everyone. While we were basically sympathetic to the socialist ideals espoused by the new regime, we did not in any way approve of the underhand brutal way they had seized power. The first coalition government should have been allowed to run its course even though there were growing concerns about the President's play-boy image and his courting of the rich and famous. He had facilitated the purchase of a large estate at Beau Vallon by a vastly wealthy man from the Middle-East who then anchored his huge yacht off Victoria. This was the first step along the road, the regime said, to selling the islands to rich foreigners, something the new government promised it would never do.

We had had our own brush with speculators earlier in the year when two men visited our rented gallery and returned the very next day with the owner. We followed them on their tour of the house and listened to their plans to convert it into a restaurant, even going so far as to notice our batiks and deciding it should be an Indonesian restaurant. The owner gave us, as tenants, the opportunity to make an offer to buy the property. We thought, with the help of the bank, we could scrape together twenty thousand pounds, while the speculators offered twice that much. We were put on notice that we would have to move on once the sale was finalised.

Peter, the architect, was at that time working on a project at Mare Anglaise to the north of Beau Vallon. Vacoa Village was to be a cluster of self-catering apartments with a restaurant and swimming pool. We talked our way into the plans and Peter designed a purpose built gallery with living accommodation above. Building had commenced when the coup took place and the dilemma we now found ourselves faced with was what to do about this half-built gallery. Did we give up and leave, like so many other people, or did we sit it out in the hope that the new government would change things for the better? In the end, because of the legal implications, we decided to stay.

We moved into our new house and gallery towards the end of that year when Vacoa Village had started operations. Peter and Linda had meanwhile pulled out of the so-called Sheraton project and had emigrated to the United States.

The house at Beau Vallon that we had vacated never did become an Indonesian restaurant, the investors had fled and the house was acquired by one of the ministers in the new government.

While so many aspects of the new regime seemed to be making the situation worse, like threats to nationalise all foreign-owned hotels and even private property; it came as a pleasant surprise to hear that Knud and Gisèle had moved into an impressive old house known as Bagatelle. The house with its beautiful garden was on the Sans Soucis road, but closer to town than their previous homes. It was a house with an interesting history, having been built using all the timbers from an old sailing ship with the same name.

It seemed as though they had moved up in the world, living in this large house, furnished with their antique furniture and enjoying the peace of the garden and the view of Victoria. Financially better off because of work from the Italians, the hard times of the last few years seemed to be behind them.

Knud was in an expansive mood after several visits to his office at home by an American entrepreneur. This newcomer had been attracted to Seychelles by rumours of our rapidly developing status as an international tax haven which had probably been started by the previous government and were now fostered by the new one, despite its anti-capitalist rhetoric.

'Uncle', as Knud called him, was proposing to build the headquarters of a new World Bank in the Third World. He had, on his own initiative, chosen the ideal location on the mountain top below Mont Blanc in the middle of the national park. Somewhere high up, so that it could receive all those modern electrical signals, and secluded enough to ensure its security. Knud was to be the architect, chosen to design a Shard-like glass tower ideally suited to such a pie-in-the–sky scheme.

It seems that 'Uncle' had been to put his proposal to the relevant department but it proved to be too much of a capitalist dream for our new

Cuba-centric government. At the end of his holiday in the tropics, 'Uncle' was never heard of again.

At the other end of the scale was Alice, our boiler-out-of-wax and now sometimes gallery attendant. She lived at St. Louis in a very modest little cement block house with a corrugated iron roof. The house was on a piece of land rented from one of the Grand Blanc families. Her husband, a retired fisherman, two grown-up sons and a nephew, plus two illegitimate grand-daughters shared the house with her.

Alice was fiercely matriarchal and kept her home and family on a tight rein, ensuring that her grand-daughters received a proper education. One son was a policeman and the other, the apple of his mother's eye, a bit of a drifter and responsible for producing the two grand-daughters. Despite a very strong Catholic background, it was socially acceptable to have children out of wedlock – young men seemed to stay with their partners until the inevitable conception occurred and then absconded and abandoned them. The stronger-willed grandmother got the children.

The socialism and promises of the new government were meant to appeal to families like Alice's. After all, there was a new edict that allowed tenants of property owned by large landowners the right to have the land surveyed and the rent they were paying would become payment for the purchase of the land and house. Like many Seychellois, Alice was very ambivalent about such promises.

Despite, or maybe because of the uncertainty, we decided in April 1978 to have a look at the USA. We collected Grandma from Lytham and took a flight from Heathrow to New York. We liked the museums, Central Park and the hustle and bustle, the steam coming out of the manholes as it does in the movies. We admired the Empire State Building, the UN headquarters and saw the Statue of Liberty across the water. We hired a car that we could return at the airport in Los Angeles after we had driven right across the country.

The car was a Plymouth Fury and

after the modest vehicles in our lives, it felt as though it was a hundred feet long and fifty wide. It was, to put it mildly, a frightening experience to emerge from the underground garage into the speeding traffic on a busy New York street with only the vaguest directions given us by the attendant. Once we were over the bridge and motoring along the highway or turnpike or whatever it was called, we calmed down to a sedate fifty miles per hour which was the speed limit. We had driven about 100 miles before we needed to make a stop at a gas station to fill up and visit the rest rooms. The attendant was busy pumping what seemed like hundreds of gallons into the tank, smiled at me and said, "You folks sure have come a long way."

"Yeah!" I said, wondering how to explain where Seychelles was.

He looked down at the number plate, and with a shake of his head, added "I've never been to Philadelphia myself."

Everyone told us to have a nice day, which we tried very hard to do and even people we had hardly spoken to asked us how we were today, and told us we were welcome, which was a relief.

We made slow but steady progress across the country in our car that felt like a flying bedstead, every night stopping at 'Sleepy Bear' motels with their identical rooms and furnishings and every day consuming obesity-inducing meals. Our leisurely fifty miles per hour took us down to Washington DC where the White House was larger than our little capital, Victoria.

We wandered through the Shenandoah Valley and out across the vast mid-west. In a restaurant in Oakley we were treated to the first edible steaks of our journey, but Grandma was a little taken aback when she complained to the elderly mini-skirted waitress that the coffee she had just served was cold.

"Oh! Really?" said the waitress and went off to pour cold coffee into someone else's mug.

The Nevada desert was a stunning contrast to our tropical island landscape – not a palm tree in sight. We felt more at home in the Rockies on our way to pueblo Indian country and a pilgrimage to D.H. Lawrence's grave.

A day or two later, as we stood awestruck on the rim of the Grand Canyon, remembering that in our tiny group of islands every island, bay, headland and rock is named for someone in the history of the islands, we heard a nearby guide bellowing out a list of statistics to his group and then, with rising excitement, pointed to a towering stack of rock, exclaimed, "And over there is the Snoopy Rock!"

Thus brought down to earth, we trundled off to Boulder with its huge dam and a main street full of car repair shops, hairdressers, furniture stores and diners, in no particular order. We found a restaurant where we sat in an orchard of plastic orange trees.

In the City of Angels, we finally found the technical wizardry we had not found anywhere in the States – at Disneyland. And finally, the crowded six lane highway to the airport made us long for the winding little coast road that led to the Seychelles airport.

A month later we returned to Seychelles and found ourselves in a totally new political world. The President had declared that henceforth the country would not tolerate political opposition and thereby instigated a one-party state. He would choose his own ministers and rule by decree. Twenty Seychellois, who he deemed to be a threat to his political ambitions, had been arrested and imprisoned at the Union Vale prison.

One of the detainees was Alix's father, Felix, who was later released and took his family into exile in the U.K. As if the sudden departure of Anna and Alix was not sufficient notice that unwanted changes were about to be forced on us, the new Education Minister decided that from the start of the new school term in January, Seychellois children or children of naturalised Seychellois parents would no longer be allowed to attend the International School. From that date children would have to enrol in their local district school. In our case, this was a single class of children between the ages of six and twelve. Parents were not permitted to supply pens, pencils or notebooks or similar elitist paraphernalia – these would in future be supplied by the state to be shared equally by all the children.

We thanked our lucky stars that we had managed to get the Yorkshire barn conversion completed because there was no way we could sacrifice Justin's chance of a good education for the vague hope that we would have a better future in the islands.

Taking a gamble, we booked our passage on a cruise liner that was to call at Seychelles at the end of October and was bound for Southampton at the end of its Indian Ocean cruise. When we had spare time in those last months, we spent them with Justin on the reef flats at low tide, looking for shells, watching the fish and crabs in the pools and admiring the sea anemones and corals.

In the evenings we mostly worried ourselves into a sleepless state, worrying about disposing of the gallery and the stock of pictures and beachwear. We needed the income from the gallery and if possible, rent from the flat until we found our feet in Yorkshire.

At the eleventh hour we had a call from an Italian painter who was interested in buying the whole building. We showed Renzo and his wife, Lydie, around and accepted the offer they made. We knew them fairly well so that when they offered a cash deposit and the balance as soon as possible, we made arrangements to have a contract drawn up by a lawyer. It all seemed very much above board; Renzo was expecting funds for a sculpture the new government had commissioned for the roundabout at Independence House. He felt totally secure about the future, probably because he had a friend who was one of the central members of the regime, and thought that we were being over-anxious about our future in Seychelles.

Gisèle and Knud also thought we were over-reacting but understood that our primary concern was for Justin. Other friends like Pauline and Chris, whose children were not affected by the new dictat, decided to stay on. Peter and Linda had already left for the States and Russell and Jill, the potters, had returned to South Africa. Guido and Ada had closed the Tartaruga Felice and gone to Spain. Most of the colonial service people we knew had left at Independence and so it was not too difficult for us to join the exodus.

Alice was very upset when we told her of our imminent departure. She had become an important part of our small enterprise and spent her last few working days clutching her prayer book and praying for us.

When the 'Vistafjord' docked we were packed and ready to leave. One advantage of travelling on a ship was that we could store all our belongings in the hold all the way to Southampton.

It was a fascinating voyage that took us to Mauritius, Madagascar, the Comores, Dar es Salaam, Zanzibar, Mombasa, Aden, Port Sudan and Cairo, while the ship transited the Suez Canal. We travelled through the Mediterranean to Gythion in Greece, then Genoa. While the ship was refuelling there, we went to see Marisa and Abramo, old friends of Gill, who had made the contact for us at the Galleria Il Punto the previous year.

Thoughts of the approaching winter in North Yorkshire had prompted Gill to ask Marisa if there was anywhere we might purchase a pair of fashionable Italian-made boots on a Sunday morning.

We four adults, plus Justin, set off at a leisurely pace in Abramo's little Fiat 500 to Santa Margarita, on the autostrada along the coast from Genoa, where Marisa's friend had a shoe-shop which she would open especially for us.   Driving along the motorway, Abramo was telling us about his work translating into Italian the comics of Topolino (Mickey Mouse) when he realised he had passed the exit from the autostrada. Nothing daunted, he stopped, put the car in reverse and took us zooming backwards against the flow of the traffic, setting off a cacophony of hooting, shouting, and expansive Italian gestures until we regained the exit slip-road. The chaos that he'd caused didn't seem to phase him in the slightest. "They only make rules so that you can break them" was his philosophical comment.

Santa Margarita was a charming little port in a sheltered bay and while Gill and Marisa were busy in the shoe shop, Abramo, Justin and I enjoyed a quiet coffee in the winter sunshine. The journey back to the ship was less adventurous and Gill was extremely pleased with her 'veal' (calf leather) boots, as Marisa called them.

Thus equipped we boarded the ship again, calling at Barcelona before sailing past Gibraltar and then on to Lisbon and La Coruna before facing the extremely rough Bay of Biscay to Southampton.

We enjoyed ship-board life with its institutional meal times and someone else to wash the dishes and make the beds. Most of all we attended all the talks given by Hans and Lotte Haas who had spent so much time diving in the Red Sea.

Cold winters and Spanish sunshine

It was so cold that first winter in the Yorkshire dales. Our internal thermostats had, over the years, reset themselves to tropical temperatures where twenty degrees centigrade at night was reason to get out the thick blankets.

We had invited Grandma,

Steve and Stephanie and their two girls, Kathy and Chris, to spend this, our first family Christmas, together. They came with the first flurries of snow that promised the white Christmas we tropical exiles only dreamt about. The snow kept falling until even the tops of the dry stone walls on either side of the roads disappeared. It was as well that we had prepared for the seasonal over-indulgence as the roads remained blocked and the village snowbound for several days.

Despite the snow, life had to go on; like the hyacinths and daffodils that were pushing their first shoots above ground, we dreamt of the coming spring. The local primary school that sat on the hill between Malham and Kirby Malham was pleased to accept Justin and we settled down to our version of village life. We introduced ourselves to the neighbours and got to know the families on the adjoining farm and went for walks to the famous Cove that we could see from our bedroom window. We soon learned that it was best to stay in the walled garden on summer weekends to avoid the crowds of walkers from the cities.

During the summer we had a visit from Auntie Heidi and Harry from South Africa, who enjoyed being driven around the dales and seeing the little villages. It was one of those periods in summer when the interminable grey skies won't rain, nor let the sun shine through. Ever the optimist, each time a penny-size area of blue sky showed itself, Heidi would point and say, "Don't worry, it's clearing, my girl!" It did eventually, but they were long gone by then.

What we desperately needed though was to find a way of supporting ourselves. We had a substantial list of names and addresses of people who had bought our craft work in Seychelles and we thought we could use this to set up a mail order business. There wasn't room in the house to set up a workshop, but we had plenty of space in the old adjacent walled garden. It was necessary to get planning permission to breach the garden wall and to install a Portakabin within the enclosing walls. Once we had it wired and the plumbing connected, we had plenty of room to do the waxing and dyeing. It was just a pity the response to our mail shot was so slow.

There was a long strong thread, like the silk spun by the golden orb spiders, that bound us to Seychelles. A little bundle of letters from our post box in Victoria arrived once a month, accompanied by a few scraps of news from Gisèle. She told us that there had been demonstrations in Victoria against the President's introducing a Cuban inspired National Youth

Service which would take most of the teenaged children out of the family environment to spend their school terms in the facilities specially built for them on St. Anne Island. It was a move seen by many parents as a way of politicising the children in the mould of the regime.

That Justin wouldn't be subjected to such obvious political indoctrination was a relief. Much better that he should have a normal childhood and only have to worry about more important problems like why his headmaster needed both a fork and a spoon to eat spaghetti, when everyone else he know used only a fork!

The news we really wanted from Seychelles was that Renzo had made the final payment for the Vacoa Village gallery but he always had a reason to procrastinate for just a little while longer. Some news we had not expected came in the form of a brief note from Guido and Ada who had opened a restaurant in Spain and suggested that we should look at the possibilities there too.

That was what we did in October. We found a two-week package that covered the flight and accommodation in a house at Nueva Andalucia, outside Marbella. We found ourselves within walking distance of Puerto Banus where Guido and Ada had opened their new Italian restaurant 'La Tortuga Feliz' (the Spanish translation of their old 'Tartaruga Felice'). We sat in the warm autumn sunshine on their terrace, admiring the expensive yachts and listening to their enthusiasm. We were suitably impressed by the port and its possibilities. The restaurants were not that expensive, even in Puerto Banus, and in the supermarkets, good wine was so cheap that we could have wept for Gisèle and the price she paid for the acidic plonk she drank.

The Spanish autumn sunshine was the prelude to the frost and snow in Yorkshire. The roads across the tops to Settle were closed, the landscape an unblemished silent world of white, even the birds must have been huddled together trying to keep warm until the thaw. The dull grey sky and bitter cold kept us indoors, gathered around the open log fire, dreaming, as ever, about the sun and the warmth.

<u>A gallery in Spain</u>

Located as it was in this picturesque little Yorkshire village, so close to Malham Cove, the barn soon attracted a buyer. We took Justin out of school, put him in the back of the car with his school books and a pile of Tintin and Asterix books, and set off for Spain. The house we rented was well equipped, spacious and newly-built, with a swimming pool and only about one hundred metres from the beach.

In Puerto Banus we found a vacant shop facing three restaurants that opened onto a small square. It was vacant in the sense that it had been waiting to have the windows fitted, the floor laid and the

walls and ceiling plastered. Once all the legal stuff was completed, we found a contractor to do the plastering and painting and to lay the white marble floor tiles. Pepe, the builder, with only one remaining tooth in his mouth, said that work on the gallery would take four or five weeks which gave us sufficient time to return to London to meet my parents who were due to arrive at Heathrow from Johannesburg. They had come to Europe for the first time in their lives and we had offered to take them around England and across the Continent to Spain. Mom had always been an avid reader and was pleased to see the places she only knew from books. Her only disappointment was the 'money lenders', as she
called the money-making souvenir stand in the heart of St. Paul's Cathedral.

Our tour started with visits to Gill's family, then we drove through Bronte country with a day or two across the English countryside to the Channel. My father was more interested in technology than architecture, so we treated them to a channel crossing on the Hovercraft, much to his delight; the rolling and surging on the rough sea did not please Mom.

We drove through Belgium and across the Rhine to Heidelberg so that my father could see a little of the country where his parents had come from. Our southward journey cut briefly into Switzerland and then across France towards Spain. We made a memorable stop at the Pont du Gard where one of us, who shall not be named, over-indulged on the crop of fresh cherries, necessitating a two night stop to recover when we reached the Costa Brava in Spain. We took two more days to drive along the Mediterranean coast as far as Marbella and the house a few kilometres beyond San Pedro.

My parents had only a few days to recover from the long car trip before we took them to Malaga airport at the start of their homeward journey.

To celebrate the opening of our smart new gallery we had invited a small party of friends. Guido and Ada came with another couple we knew from Seychelles, Haldon and Jenny and their friends, Tom and Ruth, who had a shop further along the Port. The walls were hung with our best and brightest batiks, all lit up by an array of spotlights which, coupled with the party atmosphere would, we hoped, attract the attention of the many diners in the posh restaurant that faced our gallery across the square.

It felt as though we had reached an important milestone in our lives. Here we were in our own pure white, minimalist gallery in the heart of Puerto Banus with its expensive shops, its fancy yachts, flash cars and smartly dressed people, and only a few kilometres from Marbella, home to the rich and infamous.

There was a lot to learn about running a gallery in Spain even when we only sold what we had made. We needed a 'gestor' – a commercial lawyer – to sort out the bureaucracy. Frequent visits to his office in Marbella usually involved hours of thumb twiddling and staring at the wall, only made bearable by thoughts of the cake shop on the street below his office. It also took a while for us to adjust to the Spanish shop hours. There was no point in being open before twelve noon and after two o'clock was siesta time. We generally reopened about four in the afternoon and worked until eight or nine except in summer when the Port was busy until late, then I stayed until around midnight.

On long summer nights we had our first inkling that Puerto Banus might not be the best place to sell handmade craftwork. It was a very ostentatious place, a place where people wanted to be seen and where money was spent on showy fashionable clothing and finery, not on cotton kaftans, sarongs and batik paintings. On those long summer nights when the restaurants were so busy that they spread themselves across the square, the late diners used to sit on our flower boxes waiting for a table, but they never ventured across our threshold.

It took twelve consecutive months of not making enough money to cover our monthly expenses before we realised that the gallery in Puerto Banus was not the right place for us. On the other hand, we really liked Spain, especially this part of Andalucia with its warm friendly people and the beautiful mountain scenery and white villages along the road to Ronda, or down the coast to Gibraltar. Tom and Ruth were an endless source of information about the countryside and the most interesting towns and villages to visit, but best of all, they seemed to know every restaurant and bar worth visiting along the way.

Justin seemed happy at Calpe College, the small international school on the outskirts of San Pedro. Larga, the baby dachshund we had bought, had settled into her new life, even coping with a very busy house in summer when we had a constant stream of friends and family to stay. In the autumn after all the visitors had left, we needed to move to a smaller house with a more affordable rent. Our new residence at Monte Biarritz was in an 'aggrupada' a single terrace of holiday homes in a large communal garden with a swimming pool.

We had an unresolved problem to deal with in Seychelles, the unpaid debt for the sale of our gallery there to Renzo. The obvious solution was to spend the money on a short visit to see if my presence on his doorstep would resolve the matter. It didn't; he was very apologetic and made further promises when I talked about legal action. The most positive outcome of my visit was to establish an outlet for our batiks in Haldon's shop at the Coral Strand hotel.

Gisèle had offered to put me up for the duration of my visit and was pleased to have my company in the evenings as Knud had taken to retiring to his bed quite early. They had two exciting novelties in their lives: Knud was very proud to have been appointed honorary Royal Danish Consul and Gisèle was delighted to be the proud owner of a television set. The government had finally decided to add a television service to the state-controlled radio station.

One day, early on in my visit, I went to see how Alice and her family were getting on. I was greeted like some long-lost family member and to my question, "Comment ça va, Alice?" she replied with her usual,

"Pas plus mal, Monsier Ron." (No worse!)

Alice made me promise to call again before I left as she had something I should take back for Justin. It turned out to be a model of a small cargo vessel called *Nordvaer* which was too fragile to consign to the hold on the flight and too big for the overhead lockers. I sat squeezed in between two other silent grumpy-looking passengers throughout the long flight and ate my meals peering through the boat's rigging, all the way from Seychelles to Malaga.

The survivors' guide to rebellions

There was an obvious compromise we could make: enjoy our lives in Spain but support ourselves by exporting what we made to Seychelles where we still had a market of sorts. We decided that it would be worthwhile spending the end of the year school holiday period working in Seychelles. This would enable us to build up enough stock to cover several months of hoped for sales. When we told Haldon and Jenny over a pork fillet lunch at El Sarten in Benahavis, they offered us the use of their house and studio at Danzilles for the duration of our stay.

It was late November and we had only been in Seychelles a few days when frantic phone calls, first from Gisèle and then Pauline, alerted us to the news of what sounded like yet another coup attempt. We switched on the radio and were informed that there was an armed confrontation at the airport. That was all the information there was, other than wild rumours that spread from house to house. We learned some time later that the exiled politicians had realised that diplomacy would not bring about a return to democracy and had decided to mount a counter-coup. The driving force behind the exiles was reputed to be Gerard Hoarau, the ex-chief immigration officer who had listened to me swearing my Oath of Allegiance to the Queen eight years previously.

The exiles turned to the ageing Irish ex-Congo mercenary, 'Mad Mike' Hoare, to recruit around fifty men in South Africa. He put together a mixture of young guns and his old comrades in arms, now running to fat and wanting one more rush of adenaline. These mercenaries flew into Seychelles as the 'Order of Frothblowers'; a charitable beer-drinking group was a bizarre choice of cover. They had a happy time drinking on the plane and swept through the airport until the very last of them was stopped by an observant customs officer. At the bottom of a bag of toys supposedly intended as gifts for children a gun was found.

Chaos ensued and shots were fired, rather wildly as only the walls of the control tower were hit by anything. Realising their plans had gone awry, half the group headed one way and half the other. One lot hijacked a refuelling Air India aircraft and escaped to South Africa, but the others headed inland. No-one knew exactly how many mercenaries were still at large on the island, or where they had gone. Road-blocks were set up and the army, most of whom were Tanzanians, seemed to be everywhere.

We were all told to be vigilant, to stay at home, to report any unusual men who might turn up in our gardens. Instructions about when to go out and restock would follow. Our survival guide remembered from parental wartime stories was: one, to fill the bath with water in case the water mains were blown up. Two, put candles in strategic places and keep matches handy in case the electricity fails. Three, check on food stocks to see what could be made to last or could be used imaginatively, like using custard powder to make chapattis!

The following morning we had another frantic call warning us that one of the mercenaries was in the forest somewhere near Danzilles. We locked the doors and decided where we would hide if anything nasty were to happen. Fortunately it proved to be a false alarm and four mercenaries were taken prisoner and were going to be put on trial. The curfew dragged on as there seemed to be one unaccounted for. Finally lack of food became too much for him and the last of the 'Frothblowers' surrendered himself without incident.

The next six weeks were devoted to waxing and dyeing as much fabric as we could afford. Alice was happy to do the boiling out at home. She used a 'fer blanc' which was a large square container in which cooking oil was imported. This was balanced on cement blocks over an open fire. The final rinsing and washing she did in the stream that ran along the side of her house. Our two sewing ladies, Daphie and Noemi, were pleased to get the extra work. The only problem was having a very limited space in Haldon's busy shop.

Quite by chance we heard that there was a small shop available at Beau Vallon. Marghita, the wife of George, who had been the mechanic present at the death of our VW Kharmann Ghia, was the family agent for the shop. It was somewhat dilapidated and in need of paint, but had a large window facing onto the main Beau Vallon road and was opposite the Sea-Crest beach-side bar and restaurant. When we put it to Alice that we could offer her full-time employment as our shop assistant, she was all smiles and dashed into her house to find her prayer book.

Back in Spain

We collected Larga from the boarding kennels, her wagging tail proving that she was much happier than the "why did you leave me?" look on her face indicated. We resumed our Spanish lives, trips out to see interesting places or to watch the storks returning to their bulky nests on old buildings or even electricity pylons. Tom had found us a new restaurant, 'The Wide-Mouthed Frog' where the English owner was heard asking the golfing holiday fraternity: "Who ordered the overdone steak?"

Out of curiosity we often went to look at the weekend Rastros – open street markets – to see which crafts were new or interesting, or to buy second-hand books. That was where we met Sonia and Hermione, sisters who owned a bookshop in Estepona. They were also heavily involved in animal welfare. For obvious reasons, we never told them of our visits to the bullring at Nueva Andalucia. In my earlier life as a hitchhiker in Spain in 1960, I had been an aficionado, probably carried away by Hemingway's passionate interest in the corrida.

My interest had begun to wane when we saw some fights descending into unnecessary brutality and the theatrical arrogance of the matadors was brought down to earth by Gill's pointing out the holes and ladders in their stockings.

When we returned to Seychelles six months later, we sensed that there was a certain ambivalence towards the government. Many of the people who felt disenfranchised politically by the one-party-state had rallied around the government after the ridiculous mercenary affair. It was a feeling of support for the country, rather than for the government. There were many good social ideals worth supporting that were intended to make life better for the majority. On the other hand, so many middle class educated people had emigrated after the coup, making it difficult to find qualified people to run the nationalised hotels, businesses and state farms. It soon became obvious that these posts were going to political cronies with little or no experience.

Gisèle had found us a house to rent at Mare Anglaise, overlooking Beau Vallon and within walking distance of our shop. We had planned to work seven days a week for the next six weeks to ensure that there was enough stock to last for several months. Alice was happy to fill in for us if we needed her but otherwise, continued to do the boiling out at her own pace at home. For our part, we had set up a primitive but functional workshop in the small yard at the back of the shop.

Knud was still being kept busy by his Italian benefactors who were well in with the President. With an assured but by no means excessive income, Knud had more or less given up on regular meals in favour of support for Seybrew – the local brewery. The result was that when Gisèle entertained us, we were treated to her considerable culinary skills. Knud sometimes joined us at table with a token gesture on his plate and a glass of wine at hand to help his digestion. Mostly he sat in his wing-chair and read, or told us tales of his days in Kenya, Zanzibar or Somalia.

The school holidays were drawing to a close and we were starting to make plans for our return to Spain. It was August, the sun had barely crept over the mountain behind the house and begun to spread its warmth across Beau Vallon beach, when the phone began to disturb the peace. It was Gisèle.

"Stay where you are. Don't go out. I can hear gunfire and there is a lot of activity at the army residence in front of our house."

"Oh shit! How could this happen?" This was our fifth coup, if we counted the fiasco in Spain the year before when General Tejero tried to take over the Spanish parliament but was thwarted by the intervention of King Juan Carlos.

But it wasn't actually a coup this time, it was called 'an army rebellion'. The President was away on one of the outer islands on a fishing trip. A group of soldiers, dissatisfied with their conditions and with always playing second fiddle to the large contingent of the more trusted Tanzanian military, had decided to take matters into their own hands. An immediate curfew was imposed and they managed to take control of the radio station. They claimed to be holding many hostages against retaliation from the Tanzanians and those members of the local army and militia loyal to the government.

The radio had always been an important part of everyday life in Seychelles. It was used to inform the public of recent deaths, funeral arrangements, calls for stevedores to report for duty at the port and general community activities. It was a vital link for families living on the outer islands, sometimes on a quite personal level. It made perfect sense therefore for the rebel leaders to try to send a message to the President over the radio to assure him that they still respected him, but wanted some of the senior members of the army, and the Tanzanians, dealt with. There was a deathly silence from the President and this made many of us wonder if he had abandoned ship.

By the second day the rebels had been broadcasting continually for twenty-four hours and had even encouraged people to phone in with their own grievances. They appealed for the public to gather outside the radio station to demonstrate and show their support. This was very confusing because as far as we were concerned we were still under curfew. One of our neighbours had ventured out during the day. He was nervous about being seen out but had brought us a fish from his freezer in case we hadn't enough food.

At one point there was a disturbance at the Fisherman's Cove hotel, which we could see from the house. Through binoculars we saw people rushing down to the beach and taking shelter below the sea wall. Apparently a heavily armed group of rebels had arrived in a great rush, brandishing their weapons, and were rumoured to have broken into the hotel safe.

And then it all came to a sudden end. The head of the army came on the radio to say the rebellion was over and the culprits dealt with. The President too had decided to return, having packed his fishing gear away. Security, which had been a major concern ever since the mercenaries, was increased. More armed barricades appeared on the roads and especially on the road that went past the President's mountain-top residence at L'Exile.

The very first day the curfew was lifted we met Pauline and Chris for a much deserved drink at the Coral Strand. The children enjoyed their return to freedom on the beach while we swapped rebellion stories. Later, when we went to see how Gisèle and Knud had survived we found them in a bit of a state, having had heavy weapons and gunfire so close by.

A week later we returned to the peace and quiet in Spain.

Chapter 7

<u>A small farm in the hills</u>

As much as we liked the area around San Pedro, we found ourselves drawn to Estepona, a small seaside town further along the coast towards Gibraltar. The modern buildings along the seafront promenade gave no hint of the older part of the town spread across several low hills. The narrow streets were crowded with many traditional houses with front doors opening from the very edge of the streets onto quiet, cool, flower-filled inner courtyards.

We often made our way to Plaza Manilva where Sonia and Hermione had their bookshop. Sometimes, if we planned our day properly, we had lunch at La Fuente, around the corner from the bookshop. It was one of those courtyard houses and retained all the aspects of its original architecture. The restaurant was run by an English couple, Mike and Michelle, who on one occasion suggested that I hold an exhibition in the restaurant. I put together a small collection of drawings I had done of La Concha, the mountain that rises behind Marbella. It wasn't a great success, but I had had a great deal of pleasure drawing that inspiring landscape.

On one of our frequent visits to Estepona, we found an advertisement in an estate agent's window describing a small farm, a 'finca', not far from the town, comprising a small house and 26,000 square metres of land. We wondered if we could survive by living off the land, being self-sufficient, growing our own food and selling the crops the advertisement reported growing there.

We arranged with the estate agent to drive out and look at the property. We left Estepona by way of the Poligono Industrial, which wasn't a very auspicious start. We cut off the tarred road onto a dirt road that wound its way up the foothills of the Sierra Bermeja for about four kilometres. As we followed the curve around the top of a hill and seemed to be heading straight towards the mountain, we suddenly turned right off the main road onto a track that doubled back towards Estepona.

And there it was: a small white painted cottage looking down on Estepona and the blue Mediterranean. Inland, the Sierra Bermeja rose majestically into the clouds. The steeply falling land all around
us was covered in olives, almonds, carobs and figs. There was no sound of traffic, only the distant bleating of goats and above us the constant calling of a large flock of bee-eaters… and was that a partridge calling on the hillside? We tumbled down a wide footpath that led down to a fold in the landscape where we peered into a brick-lined well full of water.

There was no comparison between this finca and the property we had considered buying a few months earlier. That was a much smaller place on the corner of the sometimes busy Benahavis road and the road that skirted the Atalaya golf course. That property, with its run-down house and overgrown garden, belonged to Sean Connery but he had not lived there for many years. However, the hole on the golf course right opposite the house was still known as '007'.

We paid a deposit to the estate agent and left him to deal with the sale documents. Not being very good at sitting back and contemplating our next course of action, we returned to Monte Biarritz and drew some plans for the finca. Extending a rural property did not involve a long drawn out planning process which was a relief. While we waited for the agent to finalise the sale we decided to send me to Seychelles for two weeks.

There had been another nasty incident in Seychelles when I returned in December. Two men had been killed in an explosion in a car at Anse Forbans in the south of Mahé. They were said to be members of a new opposition political group, the Mouvement pour la Resistance. State media portrayed it as a self-inflicted accident but 'radio bamboo', as the local gossip was called, blamed it on the security forces.

The purpose of my visit was to persuade Renzo that there might be serious consequences if he did not settle his outstanding debt for the Vacoa Village property. We had tried earlier to get a lawyer to put pressure on him but the lawyer, who was probably friendly with Renzo's political connections, waffled on about. "The law is like a game. You need to play it carefully." What that meant was not clear to us and it definitely hadn't been a solution. My visit turned out to be a waste of time. Renzo was in Italy and Lydie said she had no idea what he had decided to do about settling his debt.

In amongst the pile of post I retrieved from our post-box I found a letter from the BBC External Services which cheered me up. I had won a runner- up's prize in their fiftieth anniversary celebration art exhibition. The theme of the exhibition was 'Nation Shall Speak Peace Unto Nation', the BBC's motto. The batik I had entered was only fifteen inches square and in fairly muted colours. It depicted a Seychellois fisherman, sitting with his dog curled up beside him, with a small transistor radio on the ground. The picture had been selected from two thousand entries, five hundred of which were from China. My tiny contribution was one of twenty runners-up to the three main prize winners.

There was another bit of good news that helped to boost my morale. The beach house diagonally opposite our shop had been vacated by the American who had rented it for many years. The rent was affordable and the location perfect. It had originally been built as a weekend beach cottage for a well-known Seychelloise lady doctor. There was a small kitchen with space enough for our dyeing trough, a large sitting room, one bedroom and a shower room and loo. Best of all, the double doors opened from the sitting room onto a veranda with a low parapet wall protecting the house from the sea.

All that was needed in the short time before my return to Spain was to bring the trestle table and the waxing and dyeing

paraphernalia from across the road, make a hanger for the shirts and kaftans and on the veranda to rig a line on which we could hang some brightly coloured sarongs. Finally, put a couple of deckchairs on the veranda so Alice could sit and watch the world pass by on the beach, read her bible or entertain her elderly friends. We also sincerely hoped that the world passing by would be drawn in by the sarongs fluttering in the breeze.

The move from the shop to these new premises took only one day, leaving me with four days to arrange the displays and hang the paintings. I gave Alice those days off work and once I was happy with the presentation, retired to a deckchair on the veranda.

The north-west monsoon wind had faltered and the sea had that glossy calm of a day in the doldrums. It reminded me of the day on which Justin had mastered the use of a snorkelling mask and seen his first view of the undersea world. It was as exciting for him as it had been for me when I learned to dive.

To master the basics I had walked into the sea, probably right in front of where I was now sitting, with Rick and two of his diving companions. When we were chest deep, we donned our diving tanks and masks and sat down on the sea bottom. Instructions were given by gesture and important hand signals explained. We surfaced after fifteen minutes and that was it – no scuba diving course, no certificate and no log-book.

We spent half an hour diving along a gorgeous shallow coral reef the next day. Several dives later we ventured into deep water to inspect the eerie wreck of the *Ennerdale*, a Royal Navy supply ship that Gill and I had watched sinking when it struck an uncharted rock in 1970.

Joining the farmers' co-op

The estate agent in Estepona phoned to say that he had completed all the paperwork and if we could pay the balance he would give us the key to the padlock on the cottage door. It was an exciting moment when we turned off the main road onto the track to the finca. All of this hillside below the track with its trees and its spring was ours! Even Larga couldn't believe her luck as she dashed off into the grass, snuffling and yelping in excitement.

"Hola!" called a voice from the top of the bank above the cottage.

Looking down from his vantage point was a wirey man with a broad welcoming smile that was completely bereft of teeth.

"I am Manolo", he told us in Spanish. "Is it you who have bought El Esparragal?"

We introduced ourselves and asked what 'esparragal' meant. He explained that it was the place where wild asparagus grew and he would show us in the spring. His small herd of goats had begun to wander off, but before he joined them he told us that he was our nearest neighbour and lived on the shoulder of the hill directly below us.

Setting out the lines for the foundations for the extension to the cottage was probably the easiest part of the work that was to follow. Most days we dropped Justin off at school on our way to the finca but overall, we managed between the three of us to do nearly all the building work. There were bits and pieces we couldn't manage such as the electrics and the roof tiling.

We needed local craftsmen for that and also asked them to plaster the outside of the building as we were fed up with the messy, time consuming chore of plastering the interior. We were rather pleased with our building when we finally finished painting it white and tidying up the terrace.

When we were ready to move into the finca we went to collect Chaka, a puppy that Guido and Ada had offered us. He was a Pyrenean mountain dog and Spanish mastiff cross, a small fluffy bundle of mischief that would, in a matter of months, grow to be a very large dog. We had delayed taking him until now, because for the previous two months we had been living in Haldon and Jenny's flat at La Pacheca on the edge of Benahavis. The flat was quite unsuitable as a venue for house-training an unruly puppy. The only animal we didn't take to the finca was Justin's terrapin which, once it had recovered from being mistaken for a hamburger by Larga, we returned to the river.

In the spring the swifts and the bee-eaters returned. There were tiny stonechats that perched on the topmost bare branches of the trees, on the lookout for insects. Manolo came with his dogs and his goats. He showed us which were the wild asparagus plants.

Below the track, near the house, there was a narrow strip of more or less flat land on which we put the cage housing Justin's rescued hedgehog. This was also a suitable place to put the two poultry arks we had made. These were long moveable chicken runs with nest boxes at one end, from which we hoped to collect eggs one day – at least that was what we had gleaned from John Seymour's book on self-sufficiency. We bought six young hens at the Rastro and nine weeks later had our first eggs.

As the days lengthened into summer, the olives, carobs and almonds looked set to make a good crop. We only had about ten well-established fig trees but these were laden with ripening fruit that would soon need harvesting.

When we were faced with the mystery of what to do with the crops, Sonia and Hermione came to the rescue.

"Why not join the Cooperative – the farmers' co-op. It's in that long low building around the corner from our shop".

And so, we became members of the cooperative. They were very helpful and explained when and how the auctions worked and told us exactly how our crops should be presented. Figs, for instance, needed to be in special shallow wooden boxes. The boxes had to be lined with fresh fig leaves, a layer of figs placed on the leaves and then a layer of leaves over the figs, followed by a second uncovered layer of figs.

Our first crop of figs looked very good, as good as any of the numerous boxes of figs to be auctioned that day. We had paid for the boxes and spent an entire day picking the most

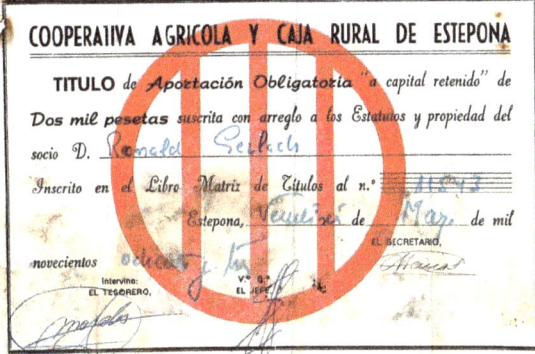

perfect unblemished figs. Our reward at the end of the auction was enough pesetas to pay for one bottle of wine at La Fuente; not the meal, mind you, only the wine.

The carob crop we sold to two neighbouring farmers for their animals. This time we could afford the meal as well as the wine. The most valuable crop, the almonds, took us several weeks of hard work to pick and haul up the steep incline to the house.

Our second crop of late season figs proved to be worth so little that we gave them to one of the other no-sale fig farmers to feed to his mula. After that Gill turned all the figs our poor tummies could no longer digest into fig chutney and jars and jars of fig jam.

In midsummer the water level in the well had fallen so low that it was proving difficult to pump the water up to the house. We solved the problem by buying a fibre-glass swimming pool and having it filled to the brim by the municipal bowser. It was an unexpected expense but it got us over the worst of the dry summer months.

One of our big worries in late summer was the wildfires that seemed to spring up out of nowhere. We had seen how frightening and fast these fires could be when we were briefly surrounded by a wildfire on the Benahavis road one day; the flames leaping like waves across the road, consuming the dry grass and rushing into the foliage of the many Eucalyptus trees. So it was with trepidation that a neighbour and I tackled a fire on the adjoining farm one day, land that was not ours but which threatened both. We succeeded but ended up a little scorched-looking and black from head to foot.

In September we knew we were heading for financial problems. With stocks low in the studio in Seychelles, Alice didn't have much to sell and there was still a substantial sum owing to us by Renzo for the Vacoa Village property. We decided to send me to Seychelles with a pile of silk we had batiked, enough to make ten kaftans.

Late on a Saturday evening at the end of October, Gisèle collected me from the airport and drove me to Bagatelle. To celebrate my arrival, Knud had opened a bottle of Laurent Perrier.

On Sunday morning Gisèle drove me to Vacoa Village to see Renzo. He was, at first, quite aggressive, but after nearly an hour of haggling we accepted that he had only two options. First, and most satisfactory for us, he could pay the whole of the outstanding debt. Second option: to vacate the property at the end of February the next year when his initial payment would have covered rent for the property. He unwillingly agreed to the first option and we arranged to meet the lawyer and get it settled before my two weeks were up.

As time-consuming as this proved to be, I nevertheless worked at the studio every daylight hour left to me. Alice was working at home and between us we produced one hundred and fifty metres of fabric, enough to keep Daphie and Noemi busy for several weeks.

There was a general political disquiet about the one party state which seemed to be following in the steps of similar regimes elsewhere. The central party clique were suddenly very well off and handouts went to the party faithful. Foreigners who did not curry favour with the ministers were finding difficulty with their development plans. The Tanzanian soldiers had been sent home after the rebellion and a group of North Korean army instructors had replaced them. On a personal level Gisèle told me she had met a Belgian, working for the Security Division, who said he knew all about Gill and me because one of his duties was to read all our mail!

Late November saw the first winter rain falling on the parched hillside at the finca. Whoever had instilled into the minds of school children the phrase 'warm wet westerly winds in winter' to describe the Mediterranean climate must have been from northern climes near the Arctic. With the winter rain came a damp cold that Spanish houses were not designed to deal with.

We were fortunate in that we had gathered a substantial pile of old olive tree logs that made a glowing, warm open fire in the sitting room. We had a portable gas fire in the hall that tried in vain to warm the bedrooms before bedtime.

Our plot of broad-beans flourished in the rain. The fold of land which held the spring that fed the well turned into a gurgling stream. In this changed habitat Justin found that we had fire salamanders living around the spring. Their bright black and yellow colouring made us wonder how they could have remained hidden from view for so long.

Lightning strikes twice

The spring sunshine put all thoughts of the warm wet wintry weather out of our minds. The pale pink blossom on the almond trees covered the hillside, every little branch on the fig trees was tipped with a fat swollen leaf bud and the vines on the terrace had begun to sprout. The swallows, swifts and bee-eaters would soon return from their wintering grounds and with luck we might see some buzzards and kites straying from the mass migration route over the Straits of Gibraltar.

One spring morning we were out looking for wild asparagus in the shrubby vegetation that covered the hill above the finca. Gill was about twenty metres ahead of me when I heard her give a gasp of surprise. Some metres in front of her, a pair of angel-sized brown wings unfolded gracefully, rising slowly above the vegetation. It was a golden eagle launching itself into the air and then looking down almost disdainfully as it gained height and circled slowly over the hill.

The wildlife so close to Estepona always surprised us. We had seen a genet – a type of civet cat - crossing the road one day and what we took to be a weasel or polecat on several occasions. We were familiar with the geckos and lizards that had shared our homes in Seychelles, but we were amazed to see a large green iguana-like lizard on the road one day. It turned out to be an oscillated lizard. On the finca we quite often heard the dogs barking frantically or, on one or two occasions, the cat hissing like a steam engine, its back pulled up into a gothic arch, tail straight up – these were the warning signs that they had found a snake. We were never sure about the snakes and generally let them be, even the two metre long grey monster that Chaka found.

Although we never heard them, we often saw nightjars rising like large overgrown moths in the car headlights at night. There was also the golden oriole that spent days in the olive trees and the beautiful bee-eaters, our most frequent visitors.

Some days after seeing the golden eagle, a remnant of the warm wet winter made an unexpected reappearance. The sky was filled with blue-black storm clouds with lightning flashing over the Sierra Bermeja. As the darkening landscape disappeared in the sheeting rain, several bolts of lightning struck the hilltop above us, instantly followed by terrifying claps of thunder that shook the house and set the dogs howling and whimpering.

Water started to pour down the wall in Justin's room, into the hall and flooding the bathroom. It wasn't until the following morning that we could assess the damage fully and try to find the leak. We found that our DIY building skills had not properly sealed the joint where the roof over Justin's room joined a vertical wall. Strange, though, that the rain hadn't found its way in there sooner.

We drove Justin to school and dashed back to start the clean-up and drying-out. The most depressing sight was the huge pile of fatally drenched books. Fortunately, the wet weather had moved on and left the warm bit behind. We had two days to get things back to normal before a trip to Malaga to collect Grandma from the airport.

At the weekend we had to deal with what seemed the almost sacrilegious task of burning the books that were beyond salvaging. Justin and Grandma tended the fire while Gill and I decided the fate of the books. It reminded me of the heretic priest Savonarola supervising the burning of books in Florence in the fifteenth century. Unlike the poor Florentines, we at least could replace our books. When the roof was repaired and the rest of the books safely stacked away from any further danger, we felt a lot more secure.

Some days when we went down to Estepona to do the shopping, Grandma would choose to stay at the finca. She would find herself a sunny spot on or near the terrace and busy herself with her knitting while sunbathing. There had never been animals in her life, no dogs and no cats and she even expressed an aversion to cats in particular. Life on the finca seemed to be the cure for her phobia as when we returned we often found her sitting with both dogs and the cat comfortably curled up asleep her feet.

We spent three busy weeks in Seychelles at the end of April making sure the studio was well stocked for the next few months. We discovered that we now had a new landlord. Government had acquired the small piece of beachside land and our studio from its German owner as part of their plans  to build a new road that would by-pass the beach road in front of the Hotel des Seychelles property.

One weekend we took some time off to go walking with Mo, a doctor friend who knew many of the trails in the mountains. We were at La Reserve in the south of Mahé, looking at the plants, when Justin found a few different species of land snail and asked what they were. I had always been Justin's source of natural history information, but this time I was at a total loss.

"Why not try the museum". I suggested. "They might have a reference collection."

Their collection was fairly limited but while he was scrutinising the snails and making notes an elderly lady, her grey hair drawn up into a bun highlighting her sharp features, leaned over his shoulder.

"Hmm. Interested in natural history, are you?"

"Yes, and conservation."

This was Betty, the best natural history guide on the islands and an inspiration to all of us.

On our return to Spain in May, Justin was preparing for end of school year exams and we were to attend a parents' meeting with the headmaster and teachers. The purpose of the meeting was to discuss the choice of subjects to be studied for O-levels. In Justin's case the subjects available were totally inappropriate for a lad who wanted to be a zoologist.

It was as though a second flash of lightning and rolling thunder signalled a change in our lives: the first, the exclusion from the International School in Seychelles and the second, this problem at Calpe College with its very limited choice of subjects. We could have looked elsewhere in Spain, but considered ourselves to be expat Andalucians, quite happy living where we did and with the friends we had made.

On the way back home we stopped in town to see Rodney, the estate agent, and asked if he would come up to the finca to give us a valuation of the property in case we decided to sell it.

In July we spent ten days in England and decided it would be good for once to live within easy reach of at least part of the family. Steve and Stephanie were living in the small Northamptonshire village of Flore in the midst of rolling agricultural land. Even the nearest large comprehensive school looked out over surrounding farmland. It seemed like a reasonable choice to make.

There were difficult decisions to make in Spain. We needed to take as many of our belongings as we could manage but at the same time leave enough so that if we could not sell the finca, we could at least use it as a holiday home – not that we liked the idea of a second home. We decided that we wanted Larga to come with us even though in those days that involved getting a rabies shot, export permits and a six-month expensive stay in quarantine kennels.

Sonia and Hermione found a kind lady with large enough grounds to adopt Chaka. We found a home for all but one of our hens. The largest, fattest hen was cooked for our final meal in the finca. The meat failed to become tender no matter how long she was cooked for, and eventually we had to admit that she was going to remain as tough as old boots and inedible. We should have let her grow old and retire from egg-laying.

Back to reality

Once we were settled in the rented house at Roade in the countryside near Northampton which Steve had found for us, we enrolled Justin at school. It was then a matter of setting up somewhere to work. It was a return to basics, the waxing frame balanced on the kitchen units and the dyeing and boiling-out in the kitchen sink.

With suggestions and some persuasion from Lisa, one of the teachers from Calpe, we did the rounds of the more prestigious shops in

London. Lisa introduced me to Paul Smith at his shop in Covent Garden who expressed an interest in our work and considered using the designs on his shirts, but that was as far as it got. We also had meetings with buyers at Liberty and later at Harvey Nicholls. The problem for us was that we couldn't even make our batiks for the price at which they sold batiks from Sri Lanka. The best contact we made was to lead to a joint crafts exhibition at the People's Gallery in Camden. When the exhibition closed in October, we were able to place all the unsold pictures and silk scarves with Liberty in the hope that they would sell.

We registered with a craft fair organisation and participated in several craft fairs in the run-up to Christmas. The venues were usually in interesting historical buildings, mostly icy cold and draughty. The compensation for being muffled up against the cold was to meet other craftspeople and have the pleasure of seeing many beautiful objects. We supplemented the somewhat erratic earnings from these craft fairs with our main source of income in Seychelles.

With this in mind I spent three weeks on the islands in January 1984. Alice had kept the studio immaculately clean and had sold the bulk of the stock. This meant three weeks of concentrated effort on my part to fill the dress rack and cover the walls with pictures.

Knud and Gisèle looked after me at Bagatelle, giving Gisèle someone different to fuss over and chatter to in the evenings and giving me a chance to think of something other than work. Knud had embarked on a new project as consultant to the government on a road which would traverse the land to be reclaimed from the sea from the airport to Victoria. His magnanimity in doing this as a free sevice to the government nearly drove Gisèle spare. As it was, they were struggling to find a steady income that would pay the rent and pay for fourteen crates of Seybrew each month.

While I was spending my days slaving over a hot stove in the humid tropical sunshine, dressed only in shorts and flip-flops, with a pinny added if I was doing the dyeing, Gill was struggling to cope with a bitterly cold winter.

The morning after I left to fly to Seychelles, Northamptonshire woke to a totally white landscape – the first snow of the season had fallen overnight together with a significant drop in temperature. Gill had passed her driving test in Seychelles some years before by resorting to tears when the police inspector hesitated about passing her. He relented but she never felt confident enough to continue driving. That is, until faced with the need to get Justin to school while I was away swanning along Beau Vallon beach. The morning after I left she found herself driving Justin to school along narrow country roads with snow drifts on either side and covered in compacted snow or, if cleared, slippery with ice. There were lorries stuck in the snow on the motorways, their drivers lighting fires to try to thaw fuel lines frozen solid by the sub-zero temperatures.

Gill's lack of confidence proved to be a blessing in disguise as she drove at a snail's pace down the minor country roads, passing the cars that had skidded off the roads and lay abandoned with bonnets buried in the snow drift. She had a nail-biting journey home with only enough time to recover before having to repeat the whole journey at the end of the school day.

There were two more days like this before the weather really closed in and the schools were closed until after my return home.

"Aren't you proud of me?" she asked when I arrived at the end of January. "I didn't get stuck once and I didn't bump into anything!"

We moved house once again in the spring. We had managed to raise a mortgage at some stupendous interest rate to buy a house in Flore, around the corner from Steve and Stephanie. It was a big improvement, especially as it had an extension we could use as a workroom. It also had a reasonably sized garden where we could grow vegetables using what remained of our farming skills.

To remind ourselves of those skills and to retrieve some of the bits and pieces that seemed to be 'at the finca' when needed, we took the ferry from Portsmouth to Santander during the Easter school holidays. Thus far we had not managed to find a buyer for the finca so we could at least use it as a base for the few days we were there.

It was too early in the year for there to be any crops to harvest but Justin was keen to bring back the two fire salamander larvae he had found in the stream near the well, so we found a decent sized glass jar to hold them on the long journey and packed them securely in a box among the jars of fig jam, olive oil and the permitted few bottles of wine.

When we docked at Portsmouth, a very officious-looking customs officer stopped us, slowly walked around the car inspecting it as though it was holding some dirty evil secrets. We were very conscious of the cars around us having to disgorge their contents. There were rows and rows of bottles of spirits and wine and cartons of cigarettes all around. He came and stood in front of the car and just stared at us malevolently through the windscreen; presumably these were scare tactics.

"Open the boot!" It was then that we became acutely aware of the two baby salamanders swimming around in their jar.

"What's in that box? Any alcohol?"

"A few bottles of wine and some opened bottles of olive oil."

He lifted a bottle of wine and very slowly inspected the label. He replaced the bottle two spaces away from the salamanders' jar, hesitated as though he might pick up another, closed the boot and scowled at me.

"Right. You can go."

We shot out of Portsmouth as fast as our little wheels could carry us, and the salamanders were none the wiser about their close shave.

Chapter 8

<u>Waiting for the Queen of Denmark</u>
There was hardly time to adjust to normal life after our return from Spain. A letter from Gisèle suggested that there was a desperate need to restock the studio. This was some six weeks before exams and end of school term, so we decided that I should go on ahead and Gill and Justin would follow when school closed for the summer holidays.

To earn my keep at Bagatelle, I agreed, despite my dismay at the militarisation of the islands, to cover for Knud at the fifth of June Liberation celebrations. He had decided that he didn't want to get dressed up and then spend hours sitting on an uncomfortable seat in the stadium.

His diplomatic status coupled with his magnanimous gesture on the road project meant that he and Gisèle were invited to join all the other important people on the grandstand near the President. And so it was that Gisèle and I found ourselves representing the Danish government and driving up to the stadium car-park with the official flag flying, to watch a tiny little island's version of a North Korean-style military parade, while Knud sat at home in his comfy wingchair, a beer or two to hand.

When Gill and Justin arrived, Gisèle could hardly wait to recount the story of the evening when Queen Ingrid of Denmark had come to visit her Honorary Royal Danish Consul at his residence at Bagatelle. Gisèle had

Our seating (circled at top left) at the Liberation Day celebarations, with our presigious view of the back of the President's head

been a-flutter for days preceding the visit, giving the house a good spit and polish throughout, washing and buffing the glasses and crockery until they looked like new and buying in a bottle of Laurent Perrier champagne at great expense.

As the hour approached, they checked once more that all was in order and that the newly washed and ironed Danish flag was in position on its freshly painted flagpole at the side of Knud's office.

Waiting for the Queen of Denmark, Gisèle would have been beautifully dressed and coiffed, her nails immaculate. She had persuaded Knud to wear his dinner jacket, something he detested. It wasn't until she made a last minute inspection of his outfit that she noticed his black jacket, which had hung untouched for decades in musty tropical wardrobes, had been chewed in a number of places by hungry cockroaches.

With little time to spare, she whipped it off him, dashed into his office, found a black marker pen and coloured in the places where the white lining gleamed though the holes. If Queen Ingrid noticed Gisèle's art-work she very diplomatically didn't comment.

Knud had his own reminder of that very special evening which he was keen to share. We all shared the bathroom that adjoined Gisèle's dressing room, but Knud had his own private bathroom on the other side of the house, handy for his bedroom and the dining room. After the Queen's visit, Knud had put a blue plaque on the wall above the loo that stated proudly, "The Queen of Denmark shat here".

We concentrated on building up the stock at the studio, gave Alice a break from being shop assistant and generally kept our sewing ladies, Daphie and Noemi, busy. Occasionally we took time off to go hiking and snail hunting in the mountains with Mo. Justin and I ventured as far as Praslin, looking for snails and, on days when we were busy, Justin took a diving course at the Underwater Centre.

The school term had already started when we returned to Flore – these were the good old days when school absenteeism was not a criminal offence and head-teachers could permit reasonable absences during term-time. We signed up for several more craft fairs, busied ourselves in the garden and took Larga on what were quite long walks for her short legs. Most of the walks took us as far as 'Dead Dogs' Field' as we called the local pet cemetery. We had the added bonus of having the family nearby and Grandma within easy reach.

There were also the theatres in London and closer to home in Northampton, as well as cinemas showing the latest films as they were released, bookshops with newly published books and records. All reminders that life on remote tropical islands was truly life on a desert island. Even in Spain where we had enjoyed many cultural experiences, our choice was limited because of gaps in our linguistic skills. These new cultural benefits were almost compensation for the rushing traffic and the endlessly grey British skies.

Seychelles hit the headlines in the U.K press in November when Gerard Hoarau, the leader of the underground Seychelles National Movement, was assassinated on the streets of London. Rumour had it that a wealthy foreign businessman, trying to curry favour with the Seychelles government, had hired a hit-man to carry out the shooting. It was never proved and no one was ever prosecuted in the U.K. But we all knew that the SNM, a disaffected group of exiles, were viewed as a threat by the one party régime. One thing was certain, the seeds of an opposition to the one party era had been sown.

Commuting to paradise

On my first journey south, away from the northern winter, it became apparent that the fatal shooting in London had not achieved what the assassin had intended. Quite the opposite. It was still a case of having to be careful of what was said and to whom it was said, but there was a determination, especially among the younger opponents of the one party regime, to make a stand for democracy.

That was the first of four trips to work that I made in 1986. We had settled into a pattern of trying to lead a normal life in England while making our bread and butter in Seychelles. We continued to busy ourselves with weekend craft fairs around the country, enjoying those that were held in stately homes a little more than when the venue was in a draughty stable block as at Lamport Hall, near Northampton.

While I was in Seychelles on a brief stay in April, the news of the disastrous nuclear accident at Chernobyl was all over the media and filled the BBC news broadcasts. My return to Flore on 3rd May gave us less than twenty-four hours to prepare for a craft fair at Lamport Hall. It was spring, the icy draughts were gone and the day started with some sun between the clouds. After we had eaten our sandwiches and listened to the latest news from Chernobyl – radioactive cloud drifting steadily westward, Gill and Justin took Larga on her lead for a walk in the Hall's extensive gardens. The clouds hastening along in their westerly direction suddenly dropped their radioactive rain on the startled threesome who came rushing back into the stable block for shelter – not a little concerned, to say the least.

On our occasional trips to Lytham to visit Grandma, we often called at Ashton-under-Lyne to see Jo and Andreas. Andreas had bought a row of garages behind their house and kept a small flock of goats in the adjoining field which produced the milk for his excellent Cypriot haloumi and feta cheeses.

On one such visit, Andreas asked about our village house in Lapithos which lay well and truly within the zone of northern Cyprus occupied by the Turks. We had no idea what had happened to our Cypriot dream. Perhaps it had fallen down in the twelve years since we had seen it? It could even have been occupied by someone from the Turkish mainland. We really didn't know. It turned out that Andreas knew a Turkish–Cypriot who wanted to return home and thought he could strike a bargain with 'a British' who had an abandoned property in northern Cyprus – like us. Andreas arranged for us call on his 'wise old Turk' who had a house on the outskirts of Manchester.

He invited us in to take coffee and sweets. After an exchange of pleasantries followed by much head-shaking and hand-waving about the Cyprus situation, we settled down to business.

The deeds and photographs were scrutinised, the plans for the conversion that I had drawn up were pored over and then we talked about the price. Andreas had insisted that we behave like true Cypriots, so we asked a rather inflated price and let him talk us down until he felt he was getting a bargain. This was not much more than we had paid for it all those years ago.

When the summer school holidays started and Justin had put all his O-level exams behind him, we returned to Seychelles for two and a half months of hard work at the studio. We were a little more independent as we no longer needed to cadge lifts or even hire a car. On my trip in April I had bought a second-hand car. It was a relation of those strange three-wheeled car of the 1960s – Reliant Robins. This one had four wheels, but no doors or windows except for the windscreen. The roof was a soft plastic cover stretched over a metal frame which kept the vertical rain out – sideways monsoon rain had free entry with a guarantee that the seats and the bottoms that sat on them got soaked. Except that it ran on petrol rather than electricity, it was more like a golf buggy than a car.

There were days when we asked Alice to keep shop for us while we trekked up in the mountains so that Justin could carry on investigating various habitats for snails. Sometimes we dropped him off at some vantage point to make his own way into the mountains.

As there were no reference books directly relating to the many species of snails that were found on the islands, we suggested that when Justin had gathered all the information and finished painting the snails, he should put it all together in the form of a small identification guide. The lady who ran the museum in the Carnegie library building put Justin in touch with Guy Lionnet, a well-known naturalist in Seychelles, who had also collected and studied the snails. He, like the people in the Natural History Museum in London, gave this sixteen year old boy access to the museum collections and treated him like a mature research student.

We had no sooner returned to the U.K. when we heard of more trouble in paradise. Although we often jokingly thought that we trailed trouble in our wake, we were definitely not responsible this time.

The President had rushed back from Zimbabwe to his island republic because he had been informed that there was an assassination plot afoot, directed not at the opposition this time but at him personally. It turned out to be some internal malaise that resulted in the head of the army resigning and three of his majors being given their marching out of the army orders.

It had all blown over six weeks later when I returned to the islands ahead of Gill and Justin who were due out in December. Knud was, if anything, even more sympathetic towards the government. This was partly due to his having embarked on a new project for the government to design a dry-dock and a naval quay. This latter project was to accommodate the navy's two small patrol vessels and the 'modestly luxurious' presidential yacht.

A book full of snails

The time we spent in Seychelles never seemed to be long enough. We always managed to fill our days doing the waxing and dyeing, keeping the studio open all week and fitting in the odd excursion. However busy we were, there was always time to enjoy the surroundings. The ever-changing ebb and flow of the tides came hissing across the powder fine sandy beach. At times during the northwest monsoon the wind piled the sea into wild waves that came crashing against the studio's veranda wall. But when the sun shone and the swimsuit-clad tourists sauntered by hand-in-hand, cheek-to-cheek in intimate conversation, we remembered why we had first come to the islands of love.

March saw me back in Seychelles after only ten weeks in Flore. The brief stay at home had been marred by a rushed trip to Spain when news came that someone had broken into the finca. We tidied up the mess, changed the lock and repaired the damage as best we could. We decided that, stuck with an unintentional holiday home, we should visit it more often to avoid giving the impression that it was abandoned.

Considering that we had left the bourgeois world with its lust for money and possessions some twenty years ago, we seemed to have rejoined it with a vengeance. We now owned a half-sold village house in Cyprus, a farm in Spain, a car and house in England (well, that part of the house not owned by the mortgage company) and another car in Seychelles.

Then there came a phone call from Andreas. The Turk, he informed me, had decided to buy the house in Lapithos. He had apparently sent a family member to look at it, or so he said. Some days later we signed an agreement in front of a notary in Manchester and he presented me with a cheque for the full amount. We decided to use the money to pay for the printing of Justin's snail identification guide.

With the end of the school year approaching, we began to think about university applications for our budding zoologist. In our modest way and not wanting to aim too high, we suggested to the headmaster of his large comprehensive school that we wanted Justin to apply for entry to Oxford, based on his successful 'O' level results.

"I'm not sure about that", he said, the creases of concern furrowing his brow.

"We've never had a student apply to Oxford or Cambridge."

"Well, we think he should apply"

There was a pause for him to weigh this up.

"Yes", he said "Why not?"

The snail book arrived in ten heavy boxes a few days after I had returned to Seychelles, meaning that I avoided having overweight luggage. That task, of transporting as many books as made up the maximum luggage allowance fell to Gill and Justin when they came out at the end of term.

We organised a small party at which to launch the book, inviting friends and those who had helped with advice and excursions into the mountains. The local press gave Justin good coverage in 'The Nation'. Later in the week, Pat, a local naturalist, who worked as a reporter at the television station, interviewed Justin for the television news.

As a reward and a birthday treat for Justin, we booked a day trip to Silhouette island. Shrouded in clouds, the island lay like a dark shadow on the horizon. The small motor yacht that we boarded made slow progress across the twenty miles of choppy tradewind-driven sea. This slow pace gave us ample time to see the ever-changing moods of the island. At times, when the sun broke through the clouds, it lit the forest-covered contours, revealing an unexpected depth to the landscape. Then, as the sun slipped behind the clouds, the island looked dark and mysterious, living up to the islanders' belief that it was home to ghosts and spirits.

This new aspect of Silhouette brought the island to life and was a foil for our romantic view from the studio at Beau Vallon where we often gazed in awe at the magical sunsets when the sun slowly sank behind this dark silhouette while every shade of orange, red and scarlet seeped into the darkening sky.

As the boat approached the island, we rounded a rocky headland, coming into more sheltered waters. We made our way along the outer side of the fringing coral reef looking for the narrow winding pass that would get us to the beach. There, hidden amidst the beach-crest vegetation were the ten thatched chalets and the bar and restaurant of the island's only hotel.

Leaving Gill sitting on the beach to recover from the plunging boat trip, Justin and I made our way up into the forest for as long as our limited time allowed. We struggled through the undergrowth looking at the plants and, as ever, hunting snails. We were back at the beach in time for a leisurely lunch and a brief visit to the old plantation house. Little did we realise at the time what an important place Silhouette would become in our future on the islands.

Our long-term plan was that once Justin was settled at university, we would return to the islands and concentrate on making a less precarious living. With this in mind, we checked the quarantine regulations with the government vet in case we wanted to import a dog. Poor Larga, after her awful detention in quarantine, had succumbed to Leishmaniasis, a not uncommon illness among animals in Spain. It transpired that as long as the dog was coming directly from the UK with its strict animal health rules, quarantine would be for days rather than weeks. This was much more satisfactory than the terrible six-month quarantine that Larga had to endure when we brought her from Spain to the UK. Within a few weeks of our return to Flore we had located a breeder of dachshunds and purchased a delightful puppy, Mitzi.

We attended the huge Anti-Apartheid rally in Hyde Park and were invited to attend a requiem for Steve Biko at St. Benedict's church – our friend Terry's parish in Hunsbury, Northampton. Terry was a long-term supporter of the dedicated work of Archbishop Trevor Huddleston and our connection with him, though very slight, took us back some twenty years.

The very best news of the year was that Justin had been invited for an interview at Wadham College, Oxford. This was followed by the news that he had been offered a place to read Zoology.

Unconditional though the Oxford offer was, there remained A-level exams to be passed at grades that would be acceptable. For this reason, we finally got around to respecting school holiday dates. Accordingly, when Gill and Justin came to Seychelles for the Easter holidays, I had already been there for three weeks, where I had been greeted with unhappy news.

Knud had been told to stop smoking as the doctors were concerned that his throat and breathing problems were a possible sign of cancer. This open diagnosis and the withdrawal from a life-time dependency on cigarettes only served to make him irritable and withdrawn. He tried his best to busy himself with work on the naval quay; the dry-dock scheme had been scuppered by the government's lack of finance.

His only pleasure seemed to be visits from Paul, the head of the navy, who often called, dressed in his naval uniform. This included a Russian styled hat that looked ten times too large for the wearer and in Paul's case, sat right down on his ears. These Russian style uniforms were meant to look tough and businesslike, but were more a symbol of Ruritania. His visits provided Knud with something positive to concentrate on. His passion for astrology, magnetism and earthquakes had become unnecessary distractions.

While we were preparing to return to the UK, Gisèle had taken heed of the doctors' advice and made arrangements for them to fly to Jo'burg where Knud could be properly diagnosed and be given radio-therapy if this were found to be necessary; as in fact proved to be the case.

For the greater part of the next two months Justin busied himself with his studies while we made plans to sell the house and car and sort out the arrangements to ship our motley worldly belongings to Seychelles. At the end of April we found another dachshund puppy - a friend for Mitzi in her new home. Max was somewhat larger than a standard dachsie and a paler colour too. Mitzi was a little confused to find a puppy sharing her bed, but soon adopted the role of Max's bossy big sister.

The shipping company had been to collect our belongings from the house for shipment to Seychelles. School was at an end and the dogs in kennels prior to being flown out a month later. With all the ends tied up and four weeks to spare before out flight to the islands, we set off with the car for a short stay in Spain. From Santander the road climbed through fields of summer flowers to the higher plateau with its vast fields of wheat and sunflowers. There were the familiar large cut-out black bulls advertising Osborne sherry on most prominent village hilltops. Slowly the road began its descent through the vineyards and olive groves of Andalucia, through the mountains to the glimmering Mediterranean.

Soon after our arrival in Estepona, we joined in the celebration of the annual Festival of the Virgen del Carmen with Hermione and Sonia.

An effigy of the Virgin was paraded through the streets carried by local fishermen and accompanied by the music of brass bands and the cheering of the crowds. Then followed prayers for all those at sea and the Virgin was taken around the bay on a flower-bedecked boat surrounded by a flotilla of small boats all sounding their horns. Although we were not religious, the dedication and enthusiasm of the people in 'our' little Spanish town made us feel part of the celebrations.

We were back in England in time for Justin's 18th birthday which we celebrated with Grandma at the Imperial Hotel in Blackpool and a day at Martin Mere waterfowl sanctuary on the Ribble Estuary. On the way back to Flore we stopped to see Anna and Alix and called in to see Jo and Andreas to pass on the latest news about 'the wise old Turk'. He had written demanding his money back. He said the house in Lapithos was a ruin and smaller than he thought.

"But we showed him all the plans and measurements" Andreas reminded me. "He even told us that one of his relatives had been to look at the property before he paid. Remember?"

"Don't worry, Andreas, the solicitor has already told me not to even think of paying"

"Good. Those Turks deserve what they get".

Four days after our return to Seychelles the vet confirmed that the dogs had arrived and were safe and sound at the vet station where they would be kept under observation for a short period. By the time they were ready for collection, we had found a house that suited us.

It was at Le Niol, about half way between Beau Vallon and Victoria. It had been partially modernised and repainted, its large airy rooms gave on to a very spacious veranda overlooking the garden and a small forest of tall trees crowded around the access road. Like most houses in Seychelles it had been built on the steep mountainside which gave it an uninterrupted view of the coastline from Bel Ombre to Glacis. The focal point of this magnificent sea-scape was Silhouette island.

It was a relatively modern house but still retained some traditional tropical architectural ideas such as having the kitchen away from the main house, only connected by a covered walkway. The garden had been neglected for a long time. The jungle of weeds and abandoned shrubs provided concealment for two truckloads of empty wine, beer and soft drinks bottles, testament, we were told, to the days not so long ago when the house had been the brothel extension to the nearby guest house.

It took some adjustment to get back into the Seychelles life-style. Temooljee's grocery shop was being brought into the modern world so that it was much more difficult to surreptitiously strip the rotting outer leaves off cabbages in order to reduce the weight. On the other hand they hadn't worked out how to keep the swarms of weevils out of the rice. We soon got used to having to float them out by rinsing before cooking this staple dietary item. Potatoes were not a substitute as they were generally ready to plant with their long sprouts, or were destined for the compost heap. Onions, on the other hand, were essential for cooking and we just put up with the three inch long growing shoots – not that we ate the shoots, we used what was left between the skin and the growing heart. Oh, it was good to get back to this organic life-style.

There were other things organic that had evolved from long-standing traditions. Nearly everyone had a few chickens in the garden from which they harvested the odd chicken curry and on occasions an egg or two, but now, with the growing population, egg farming had become a minor industry, producing fertilised eggs, some of which were fairly well developed. This was not a problem in a land where each year during the sooty tern breeding season, tens of thousands of fertilised tern eggs were consumed in a glut of orange-coloured omelettes. We felt some sympathy with the poor terns returning to find their nests empty.

Soon after we had moved into our new house, Gisèle and Knud

returned from South Africa. Knud was recovering from the radiotherapy treatment he had undergone but was still suffering the after effects. He vehemently denied that he was seriously ill, several times stressing "If you think I have cancer, well, I haven't!"

We were able to coax Gisèle out of the house for the occasional Sunday lunch at the Sunset Hotel. Knud no longer set foot outside the house.

One of the crew working on Knud's naval quay project was a navy diving instructor called Willy, a well-padded, tough little Scouser. He wife, Pam, was a diving instructor who worked with Dave and Glynis at the Underwater Centre. When it was time to take Justin to Oxford for his first term, Pam and Willy agreed to look after the house and dogs for us.

The plane landed at Gatwick at ten past five on a dark, windy and cold morning. The M25 was its usual seventy mile an hour traffic jam. Justin was duly delivered to Wadham College on time and in time for the activities of Freshers' week. Struggling to make this inevitable break, we spent two nights in Oxford in the luxury of the Randolph Hotel.

The empty nest syndrome crept up on us during those last two days. The wrench for Gill, who had had Justin's company for almost every single day of the past eighteen years, was much greater than for me, who had often been away from home. To compensate for this emptiness we took ourselves off to Switzerland for two weeks.

Chapter 9

Time and tides

There was no time to dwell on the empty nest when we returned home in November. Our concerns were all swept away when we learned that Knud had been admitted to the intensive care unit at Victoria hospital. Gisèle was trying her best not to fall apart as in addition to her fears for Knud she was suddenly aware that she could not survive on her own in Seychelles when the meagre income that had kept them afloat these past years would no longer be there.

We spent as much time as we could with Gisèle until her daughter, Jackie, arrived, taking over her affairs and helping her regain some of her composure. After the funeral, Jackie returned to South Africa having persuaded Gisèle to go and live with her. Andy came from Namibia to help her sort out her packing before they set off together for Jo'burg. The most valuable asset, the mediaeval furniture, was snapped up by Knud's Italians at a fraction of its real value but giving a sum which still represented a substantial amount for Gisèle.

In the midst of all this turmoil, my parents arrived for a two-week visit and Justin came out for the Christmas holidays. In anticipation of driving five people around the island, we had disposed of our little plastic go-kart vehicle and hired a car what was waterproof and large enough for five.

Rumour had it that the Italians had fallen out of favour with the President and were probably on their way to more lucrative fields in South Africa. This coincided with the resignation and replacement of a number of 'dyed in the wool' government supporters. To add to this minor moment of instability, the 'Economist' magazine published an article based on the government's own audit report in which it referred to the Seychelles economy as "A third world mess".

This slow, gradual change in the political climate was nothing like the other changes that had taken place during our sojourn overseas. It was only now that we were once again permanent residents and not itinerant visitors, that we noticed the changes. The famous church clock that used to chime the midday hour twice, in case we didn't hear it the first time, now only chimed once.

The old camion buses with their sometimes lorry, sometimes bus schedules and vague timetables were long gone. They had been replaced by a fleet of government owned hefty Tata buses that bore down on the traffic like huge angry rhinos, leaning perilously on the tight bends of the narrow roads. To accommodate them a new terminus had been created and the old stop at Camion Hall had become a taxi stand. The last of the vintage cars that had operated as taxis had been replaced by relatively new cars.

Food prices were under state control and the government owned the largest supermarket, 'acquired' it was said, from the family of the ex-President, and importation of all essential food items had been taken out of the hands of the merchants. Housing standards were much improved, especially for the party faithful, and the old colonial road system now carried ten times the traffic it was designed to carry.

On the road to Anse Etoile a shiny new totally characterless building was being erected where once a beautiful old creole house had stood. Men with chain-saws were amputating the limbs of a gigantic venerable Banyan tree that had shaded this romantic reminder of Old Seychelles. Many of these "old" houses were falling victim to a more affluent population. More substantial houses were also slowly replacing the traditional architecture of the workers' homes. These had usually been raised above the ground on stone pillars to keep the monsoon rain and the marauding termites at bay. Walls, doors and shutters were of rough-hewn unpainted timber planking and the roofs of corrugated iron. The kitchens were small shacks in the yard, away from the living rooms which also made the main house less attractive to rats.

Our house was quite modern in a muddled-through conversion sort of way. We also succumbed to a desire to incorporate the kitchen into the house by turning the courtyard into a large high-ceilinged room. Not long after this conversion we had

a second chance to redesign the kitchen when a tired old Bois Noir tree growing on the steep bank behind the kitchen passed away. It collapsed with a sound like a sudden gale of wind, followed by a thundering crash as it went through the roof. It seemed to me that with its view cut off by our modernisation work our ancient tree had given up the ghost and uprooted itself.

There was a new breed of expats in both the government and private sectors. There appeared to be more of them than ever before. They were mostly unaware of the Seychelles traditions of politesse based on their French heritage; standards that had been kept up throughout the colonial past. We were embarrassingly overdressed in our smart but casual dress the first time a group of these new expats invited us to dinner. They were in shorts, T-shirts and flip-flops. The old colonials would have turned in their graves.

When Justin arrived for the Easter holidays he was carrying out reconnaissance for a student expedition. He planned to bring a group of natural history undergraduates to Silhouette Island to investigate the ecology of a recently discovered high altitude endemic forest. Mo accompanied him on a four day trip to the island to sort out the logistics and find a suitable campsite.

At the end of term he was back with four enthusiastic expedition members from Oxford and added Mo and local naturalist, Pat, to the team.

We watched them board one of the island schooners, the Argo, at the port and then drove over to Beau Vallon so that we could watch their progress as they headed out to Silhouette. They spent the best part of three months camped in the high forest and we had the pleasure of acting as base camp on Mahé when they came over in ones and twos for a few days' break.

The expedition swept us along in its wake. We were drawn into the fringes of nature conservation, willingly accepting this change in emphasis in our lives. Nature had always been a passionate interest and had provided the inspiration we used in our craftwork. Our priority remained the day to day running of the studio but in our spare time we watched birds or hunted snails with Justin, or merely enjoyed nature on walks with Mo.

We made our spare bedroom a home from home for the young volunteers working on the reserves on Aride and Frégate islands. We also became close friends with Betty, the elderly lady who had inspired Justin that day in the Museum. She was the best and most dedicated nature tour guide in Seychelles and was always keen to introduce us to the contacts she made.

Betty came bounding up the steps to the house one day intent on visiting Justin's snail study room in one of the garden sheds. Staggering up the steep steps behind her, trying to keep up was a slightly over-weight, out-of-breath, red-haired man. Betty, brimful of excitement, introduced us to David Stoddard, editor of the most exhaustive study on the biogeography of the islands. He was a friendly amusing person, full of weird and interesting stories about his travels. We also knew of his involvement in the inquiry that had saved Aldabra atoll and its thousands of giant tortoises from becoming a U.S. airbase. At his instigation, I applied and was accepted onto the board of trustees that managed Aldabra.

Another of Betty's contacts with whom we became close friends was Oxford botanical artist, Rosemary Wise. Rosie was working on a book on the endemic plants of Seychelles when we met her. We went together with Rosie and Mo on a number of plant hunting expeditions whenever she visited the islands.

Of course, life wasn't all play and no work. Now that we weren't spending most of our time overseas, we were in a position to produce more batiks than we could sell at the studio. It was therefore a logical step to open a shop in Victoria. We found a vacant shop in the same building where we had run our joint shop 'Things' with Anna and Alix. We could probably even have resurrected Lady Mabs as saleslady but she was no longer in good health and in any case, we probably couldn't have coped with her sharp tongue. Instead we found Mitzi who was bright, young and enthusiastic and we could hardly hold against her the confusing fact that she shared a name with one of our dogs.

Towards the end of September, with both the studio and the shop well stocked, we took a short break accompanying Justin back to Oxford for the Michaelmas term. We included a visit to Spain to finalise the sale of our own private little piece of Spain. It was heartbreaking to cut our ties with the finca but in reality we no longer had the time to maintain the building, let alone look after the land.

Plus ça change

While we were settling matters in Spain, the first signs of open rebellion against the one-party state in Seychelles began to surface. The Catholic and Anglican churches openly criticised the government and its anti-democratic practices. The President threatened to take action against the clergy for interfering in politics, but knowing that the great majority of Seychellois were Catholics, he stopped short. Those members of the public who tried to take this further were harassed by State Security and the police.

Tourism, originally derided by the President as a route that led to a nation of waiters and cleaners, had become the mainstay of the economy; that, and the numerous licences being issued to foreign tuna-fishing vessels. The improved tourism figures were of benefit to us. The studio and the town shop were flourishing. We were able to keep Alice, Mitzi, Noemi and Daphie fully occupied.

However, towards the end of the year dark clouds settled over the island's tourism future. In August, Saddam Hussein's army had invaded Kuwait. By December of that year the Gulf War was on the brink of erupting and airlines were being warned to avoid the area altogether. This had an immediate impact on tourism with many visitors assuming that the Indian Ocean was part of the danger zone. 1991 threatened to be a difficult year. The tourists who did come were careful with their money, worrying about the future. Falling sales in the first three months and Mitzi's family problems persuaded us to close the Victoria shop.

Our increased leisure time, now that we had only the Beau Vallon studio to stock, gave us more time to devote to conservation. We made several night-time trips up into the high forest to look for the diminutive Seychelles scops owls, their rough purring calls over-riding the high pitched chirping of the tiny frogs with which they shared the forest. But most of the time we watched and counted the flocks of migratory birds.

One of the big changes that had taken place during our absence was that land had been reclaimed from the sea between the airport and Victoria. The extensive reef flats on this side of the island had been covered with sand and coral dredged from outside the reef. A two kilometre dual carriageway and an industrial zone covered part of the reclaimed land where once there had only been a narrow winding coastal road.

A string of low flat islands that now replaced the shallow tidal flats where most of the migratory birds foraged, had been planted with invasive casuarina trees. A large depression in one of the islands had been used as a siltation pond where the finer sand was allowed to settle. This provided perfect conditions for the displaced shorebirds.

When it was proposed that this area be used as a landfill site, I wrote a long letter to the editor of the government daily newspaper setting out the reasons for retaining the ponds for the birds. Much to our surprise this led to a site meeting with the then Minister for the Environment, and the subsequent registration of the first ever local non-government conservation organisation, the Nature Protection Trust of Seychelles; this was the start of our journey along the bumpy road of environmental politics.

The ground began to move underfoot for the one party government when exiled politicians formed a credible alliance and produced a manifesto for change. This call for change was reinforced when French President François Mitterand toured the Indian Ocean islands, calling for the need for true democracy and good governance. In Seychelles he publicly warned the government that if they did not abandon the one party system there would be no further financial aid from the European Union.

The President and his government, for whom one-party politics was the holy grail, suddenly made an about-turn and agreed to hold a multi-party election. Our old friend Jimmy, the first President, was allowed to return from exile to participate in the elections. He was given a rapturous welcome when he disembarked at the airport. He received an even warmer welcome from the vast crowd of waving cheering supporters at his first public rally in Victoria. My sister, Rhona, was staying with us at the time and she and Gill more or less carried me to the rally, weak and feeble in the recovery stages of dengue fever.

From that point on, it all went downhill. The one party politicians who retained power had now become reluctant believers in democracy, but only on their terms. Jimmy's star soon faded out of the local political constellation and drifted off into a world of its own. For everyone else who had pinned their hopes on him, everything had changed but nothing was different.

All at sea

To say we were thrilled when Justin graduated from Oxford is more than an understatement. Maybe we were just two more proud parents at the ceremony at the Sheldonian

Theatre on graduation day, but we were so proud of our clever kid that we must have glowed. Having graduated with a First he was to stay on in Oxford to study for a D.Phil.

It might have been that we were at the point of slipping over the edge into another generation that made us feel as though we were a replacement for the eccentric old colonials who had disappeared. Old Harry Barnsley, who had rented Lyons Corner House to us all those years ago, was no longer. Harvey, with his schooner full of holes on the Short Pier Road, had disappeared too. Even the tall, emaciated Major and his lady with the tiny dog no longer wandered around Victoria.

Gone too was the man I had met, a long time ago, on the post office steps, dressed in his pyjamas.

"I am a philatelist, a businessman", he said. "Businessmen wear suits and this is my only suit. They are clothes after all!"

When everyone had posted their letters, he would saunter off at that slow relaxed pace Seychellois had invented in this sticky climate.

Lady Mabs was probably the last to go. Although she had no known naval connections, she had insisted on being buried at sea. Even in death she was impossible to stand up to, and so, as demanded, her coffin slipped quietly overboard.

We were about to have a few adventures at sea of our own. One of the benefits of our new-found leisure time was being available to take on unusual requests.

"We have a small cruise ship on its way around the islands. Do you think you would like to act as natural history guides and lecturer?" we were asked.

The cruise ship was small, in that it carried only about one hundred passengers. Part of a fleet of Renaissance luxury cruisers, we were being asked to endure two weeks of absolute luxury, visits to remote islands, haute cuisine with free drinks, all in exchange for occasional guiding ashore and a few lectures. We couldn't believe our luck.

For one who always takes the back-seat in any conversation, the prospect of standing in front of a group of people and giving a talk was a nerve-wracking prospect. I had a large selection of colour slides of birds, animals and plants and a pile of copious notes. There were fortunately only fourteen guests on board at my first talk. I stuttered and stumbled, losing the thread each time I looked down at my notes. After the talk, an American who ran a Hollywood film publicity business beckoned me over to where he was slumped in his seat.

"Raan", he said in Californian, "You obviously know your subject very well. Take my advice and chuck your notes away and just wing it, man."

That was the best bit of advice I have ever been given. It served me well on the many subsequent expedition cruises Gill and I were invited to join.

Those early Renaissance cruises were not in any sense expedition cruises; that was to come later. The passengers tended to be uptight, wealthy businessmen and their equally fragile wives. For the first week they treated us with suspicion, finding it difficult to understand these two reserved people who were not trying to defraud them, nor even sell them anything. By the end of the first week their New York brittleness had softened and they began to relax.

We developed a sixth sense about which couples we could relate to and share a table with in the restaurant. On one cruise, on the very first day we fell into conversation with a recently widowed elderly lady and her two English/South African companions who lived not far from her in the U.S. They made a jovial threesome and we spent most of the cruise in their company. We were astounded when, a few months later, she wrote asking us if we could join her and a group of friends and family as her guests on a trip to the Galapagos islands – a naturalist's idea of heaven.

Despite all the time off from the studio, we managed to make a reasonable living. Alice, whose grand-daughters were both married, was happy with the much reduced workload and the opportunity to get out of the house on days when she looked after the studio for us. She still had a steady stream of old friends who came to share a quiet hour or two of gossip and, as always, if things were quiet, she resorted to reading her prayer book.

We were living a kind of semi-nomadic existence; a few weeks away on a ship, another spell working in the studio, trips to the U.K. followed by another fortnight sailing around the islands.

When Justin had completed his thesis, he came out to Seychelles with Laura, his fiancée, a bright, friendly girl we had met earlier in Oxford where they shared digs. They disappeared for a few days to the wilds of

Silhouette and before their return to the U.K. we made a short family visit to Bird island with its teeming millions of sooty terns.

Five years into this return to paradise we were happy and enjoying an interesting and fulfilling life. We were busy with our craftwork, our cruises and caring for the bird sanctuary we and our friends had created.

We took a month off from these not very onerous tasks in August 1994, the main reason being to attend Justin and Laura's wedding later that month. To console ourselves now that Justin was about to embark on a life independent from ours, we first spent a week in beautiful romantic Paris. We wandered along the Boule-Miche, the Tuileries, Montmartre and sat in the glorious summer sunshine on a bateau-mouche, gazing at the buildings and lovers along the banks of the Seine, dreaming.

Across the channel there were family visits to the Cotswolds where Steve and Stephanie and the girls now lived, and a trip to Lytham to see Grandma and to discuss wedding regalia. We made a stop or two on the outskirts of Manchester to make sure Anna and Alix and Jo and Andreas would be at the wedding. We had also spoken to Rosie, who said she would bring Betty. The only two people who were taking this in their usual casual stride were Justin and Laura who were busy setting up house in Cambridge.

As our presence in Cambridge was not essential, we took ourselves off to Norfolk at the invitation of Alison and Bryant, friends we had met in Seychelles when Bryant was on contract to the Seychelles Broadcasting Corporation and Alison busied herself with the national herbarium. As members of our conservation trust, they had also worked hard as volunteers on our bird sanctuary. They took us on long walks along the sand dunes along Peddars Way and also to see the waders and sea birds at Titchwell Nature Reserve.

In total contrast to our own wedding in Gisèle and Knud's garden at Mountain Rise, this was a grand affair in the historic Parish church of St. Mary in Cheltenham, Laura's home town. When Justin and Laura had changed into their 'going away' outfits and departed, I had only one more duty to fulfil – a Seychelles Bird Records Committee meeting at Tring. Then it was time to return to our island in the sun and our nomadic existence.

And then? And then along came a new alien invasive species; Australian tax inspectors. They turned many people's lives inside out, including ours, denying us all the perks we had enjoyed under the old system, and backdating this by seven years. The whole affair dragged on for weeks on end, strangers turning over every aspect of our lives. The stress was unbearable.

Almost twelve months later, after we had sold the house at Le Niol and put the money in the government's financial export pipeline, the stress was finally abating. Standing under a refreshingly cool shower one evening, I noticed what I first thought was an insect bite on my left boob. On closer inspection it felt more like a pea - a fairly small but hard pea. I mentioned this to Mo the next time we saw her. There was nothing to see and no feeling, so she arranged for me to see a specialist in the new wing of the hospital with its jaundice-yellow roof.

On the day of my appointment I arrived very early and was the first patient at the reception window. I handed in the paperwork with my details and took a seat. The waiting room rapidly filled up to over-flowing, reminiscent of the old hospital waiting room, but far less orderly. The other patients were being called up in twos and threes and shuffled off down the corridor to smaller waiting rooms.

After two hours, and approaching the time I was scheduled to attend a meeting with the Minister for the Environment, I went to the receptionist and asked about my appointment.

"What's your name?" she asked.

I told her and reminded her that I had given her my papers two hours ago. She raised her eyebrows.

"What papers?"

"I gave them to you two hours ago."

"Napa", she said with a shrug. "No papers here", sweeping her hand across an empty counter.

She slouched over to the other side of the office, dragging her feet, rifled through some papers and shrugged again.

"Napa".

In a huff I walked out and went to my meeting.

Several weeks later we were in Cambridge to visit Justin and Laura. Taking advantage of the overseas medical insurance we carried, I was given an appointment to see a doctor who sent me off to get a mammo-thingumy at the hospital. The nurse and I had a bit of a laugh about getting my washboard thin chest pressed under the scanner. The results were a rather fuzzy inconclusive picture and the doctor decided it best to remove the culprit and do a biopsy.

When I emerged from the silent dreamless world of anaesthetic-amnesia into the cosy warm hospital bed, Gill and Justin were there to commiserate and tell me that the consultant would call later to explain the radio-therapy treatment I would need once the empty space on my chest was healed. It was, I was told, typical of me to develop what was a very unconventional problem for men. Breast cancer was generally assumed to be a women's disease.

There were a few months of treatment to follow which meant staying in Cambridge for the duration. Fortune smiled on us when by some small miracle the money we had consigned to the Seychelles government's financial pipeline suddenly appeared in our bank account. We invested the funds in a small terraced house near the river in Cambridge and spent the rest of my recuperation painting and decorating.

During our absence, Alice had faithfully kept the studio open and had sold almost all the stock. On our return we plunged straight into doing the necessary waxing and dyeing in order to get the studio restocked. In our spare time we worked at the bird sanctuary or took long walks along Beau Vallon beach.

The meeting with the Minister for the Environment that I had almost missed while at the hospital all those months ago was to seek approval for the Silhouette Conservation Project. We had tacit approval from the Islands Development Company, but it all rested on the Ministry's agreement. This was granted in 1996 and we were now about to embark on a new chapter in our lives, taking a step back into life as it was lived a century ago, on an island with no roads and only 150 inhabitants. But that is a story for another time.

For us, and all who came to the islands of love, the lasting memory must surely be that of slowly sauntering hand-in-hand along Beau Vallon beach at sunset. Standing on the very edge of the Indian Ocean, the lazy waves surging around our feet. Silence. The sea is doldrums-calm, dappled with the gorgeous warm colours of the sun setting behind Silhouette.

Acknowledgements

We would like to thank Justin, Laura and Oliver for their comments and suggestions, and Robin for the discussion about the wording of the title. A special extra thank-you to Justin for dealing with the setting up process which was beyond our understanding.

www.ingramcontent.com/pod-product-compliance
Lightning Source LLC
Chambersburg PA
CBHW062110290426
44110CB00023B/2772